The Trawler
2021

Gloucestershire Poetry Society
Anthology of Selected Poems

Black Eyes Publishing UK

The Trawler 2021
Gloucestershire Poetry Society Anthology of Selected Poems
© Peter Lay 2021

Published in 2021
Black Eyes Publishing UK
50 Boverton Drive
Brockworth, Gloucester
GL3 4DA (UK)

www.blackeyespublishinguk.co.uk

ISBN: 9781913195175

All poems in this anthology remain within the copyright of the individual poets. They have asserted their moral right under the Copyright, Designs and Patents Act, 1988, to be identified as the authors of their work.

All Rights reserved. No part of this publication may be reproduced, copied, stored in a retrieval system, or transmitted, in any form or by any means, without the prior written consent of the copyright holder(s), nor be otherwise circulated in any form of binding or cover other than that in which it is published and without a similar condition being imposed on the subsequent purchaser.

A CIP catalogue record for this title is available from the British Library.

Editor: Josephine Lay
www.thegloucestershirepoetrysociety.com

Cover design: Jason Conway, The Daydream Academy.
www.thedaydreamacademy.com

Introduction

It gives me great pleasure to introduce this second anthology of poems trawled from the Gloucestershire Poetry Society (GPS) group Facebook pages. Last Year's *Trawler 2020* was a great success, and enabled several up-and-coming poets to publish their work for the first time.

So, we have repeated the process, and here are a further ninety-five poems (posted between June 2020 and May 2021) by sixty different poets. These GPS **Trawlers** are collections of poetry with a difference. Most anthologies search for poetry on a particular theme and/or tend to accept poems from already established poets. These poems have been taken from our private group which allows all our poets to post online and share their work without it constituting publication.

Some of these poems are rough first drafts, still in need of polishing (we have only lightly edited for spelling and punctuation) but never the less they are of sufficient value to be included within these pages. Some are by published poets, and some by people who have just begun writing, but each poem has an element: a style, voice or passion that called to us as we read it.

We hope you'll enjoy these varied poems posted out of enthusiasm for the written word. These GPS member poets come from all parts of England, Ireland, Scotland and Wales, from France and the Netherlands, and some from as far away as Tasmania, Australia, India, Togo and the US.

The GPS is once again thrilled to work in conjunction with Peter Lay of Black Eyes Publishing UK, and with Jason Conway of The Day Dream Academy on this *Trawler 2021.* All profits go towards funding of the Gloucestershire Poetry Society.

Josephine Lay   October 2021

The Trawler
2021

Jonathan Robert Muirhead

1978 ~ 2020

Contents

13	**A Man on the Bus**	- Laura Grevel
15	**Anew**	- Nupur Chakrabarty
16	**Any Other Day**	- Kelly Owen
17	**Apple**	- Carol Sheppard
18	**A Prayer**	- Akon Nouhry
19	**A Suitcase for Leaving**	- Sue Finch
21	**Autumnus: Roman Harvest Goddess**	- Marilyn Finch
22	**Ballad of Burg Rappotenstein**	- Laura Grevel
25	**Blood Stain**	- Matty blades
26	**Buildings (Haiku)**	- Tish Camp
27	**Circadian Riddle**	- Adele Ojier Jones
28	**Cocooned on warm sofa**	- Kuma San
29	**Contac**t	- Nick Lovell
30	**Covid City**	- Richard Adkins
31	**Creature of the Night**	- Gabby Wiest
32	**Cygnus, Monogamous**	- Catrice Greer
33	**During a pandemic, in this economy**	
		- Morgan 'I'm-not-a-poet' Rye
35	**Edge of dark and light**	- Ian Paulin
36	**Emergency Muse**	- Kezzabelle Ambler
38	**End**	- Darryl John
39	**Fibroids**	- Alby Stockley
40	**Forbidden Love**	- Gabby Wiest
41	**From Intake to Uptake**	- Chris Barber
42	**Futile**	- Anne-Marie Kurylak
44	**Government**	- Keren Hermon
45	**Hexagonal Diagonal**	- DrayZera
46	**Hollow Man**	- Keren Hermon
47	**If you liked my poetry**	- Becky Who
48	**I Just Don't Know**	- Derek Dohren
50	**In-Crowd**	- Robert Lang
52	**I see you**	- Devlin Wilson
53	**It's a lonely life**	- Scott Cowley
56	**Jennie in a Bottle**	- Darcy Royce

57	Leaving Darkness in Pine Trees Burning	
	- Franchesa Kirkpatrick	
58	**Lockdown** - Ann D Stevenson	
60	**Melness Sunset** - Jason Conway	
61	**My Darling** - Valerie Hartill	
62	**My Generation** - Nick Lovell	
64	**My ripples, My pond** - Gemma Crow	
65	**My Sofa is Missing You** - Chloë Jacquet	
66	**My stalwart friend** - Polly Stratton	
67	**New Life** - Viva O'Flynn	
68	**Not in my Name** - Clive Oseman	
71	**Nubian Queen** - Tish Camp	
73	**Numbers Are Up, So I'm Back In Covid ICU** - Lacey Tidwell	
76	**One very fucked up "I love you"** - Kelly Owen	
77	**On Hold** - Marilyn Timms	
78	**Overnight** - Sue Finch	
79	**Paroles de Joie** - Charlie Markwick	
80	**Peace** - Isobel May	
82	**Phone Box** - Carol Sheppard	
83	**Poem – Preacher – Draft 1** - Jonathan Robert Muirhead	
85	**Poetic Warning** - Becky Who	
86	**'Potential too Alluring'** - Gemma Crow	
87	**Rare Marble** - Matty Blades	
88	**Realisation** - Marilyn Timms	
89	**Salmonella Sid Stoker and Chef** - Tom Cooke	
90	**Shakespeare in the Age of Doom and Zoom** - Clive Oseman	
93	**Shapeshifters Lullaby** – DrayZera	
94	**Silence** - Sue Finch	
96	**Slept in my Dress** - Tish Camp	
97	**Spellings** - Kezzabelle Ambler	
98	**Step forward to the new year…** - Carol Sheppard	
99	**Sunday with the Dead** - Devlin Wilson	
101	**Sunrise on Cherhill** - Brian Reid	
103	**Tape my mouth** - Jason Conway	
106	**The Abscission of Trees** - Josephine Lay	
107	**The boards are bare** - Morgan 'I'm-not-a-poet' Rye	

108	**The Broken Chord**	- Trevor Valentine
109	**The Dandelion Poem**	- Trevor Valentine
110	**The Goose and the Common**	- Unknown
111	**The Keeper of Secrets**	- Clare Walters
112	**The peace of a Sunday**	- Katherine Grace Hyslop
113	**The Purpose of Life**	- Derek Dohren
114	**There's a Buddha in the Garden**	- Kuma San
115	**There's a demon roaming in the darkness of the night**	
		- Annalisa Jackson
117	**There's a monk in the kitchen**	- Kuma San
118	**There's a poem**	- Becky Who
119	**The Supermarket**	- Ben Poppy
123	**The White Discussion**	- Alby Stockley
124	**38**	- Drea MacMillan
125	**This woman feels…**	- Kay Hamblin
126	**Too many Etonians**	- Ivor Daniel
127	**Touching Carpaccio**	- Tish Camp
128	**Tournous-Darré**	- Charlie Markwick
130	**Tree People**	- Julian Roger Horsfield
131	**Versace Shirt**	- Matty Blades
132	**Virus**	- Simon Townsend
133	**War is War**	- Darcy Royce
134	**What day is it**	- John Aubrey
135	**Whispering Thoughts**	- Gabby Wiest
136	**Winter Solstice - The Oak King**	- Trevor Valentine
137	**Winter-Spring**	- Lucia Daramus
138	**You pollute me**	- Morgan 'I'm-not-a-poet' Rye
139	**Zoom**	- Suz Winspear

141   The Poets

Laura Grevel

A Man on the Bus
Inspired by poet Roger Robinson's 'A Portable Paradise'.

A man on the bus told me
to carry a portable paradise
I knew he'd say that
His belt buckle was a grinning skull
His boots flashed forked tongues
His hat was stuck with a twisted stick pin.

A man on the bus told me
to carry a portable paradise
To keep it in a paper sack
so it wouldn't be stolen
To pour it in a tin can
so it wouldn't spill out
To put it in the fridge overnight.

A man on the bus told me
it smells like the earth
After newly fallen rain
has quenched its thirst
Smells like burnt cotton candy
at the circus late at night
when the clowns have gone.

A man on the bus told me
it sounds like New Orleans
comin' down the road
A sax, a trumpet
peeling bananas
on a bulging belly.

A man on the bus told me
it looks like honey pouring
down a mountain's lips

It looks like the sunset
over your home house.

A man on the bus told me
it feels like a strong hand
that holds you through the storm
It feels like ocean bubbles
gently giggling
It feels like birth music in your heart.

A man on the bus told me
This portable paradise
would whisper the word
Would whisper the word
I needed to hear
every minute of my hours
every minute of my years
The Word!

He said his Word
Kept him upright.

Nupur Chakrabarty

Anew

The leaf is floating in the air,
the bird cooing.
This is the last time,
the final meeting, friends!
I go incognito...
far from the crowd.
I will rise anew.
You will recognize,
with a new sunshine,
will glide a known smile
and yet far from your havens,
the days shall enlighten...
a new anchorage,
and there I shall be
when time gathers the strains.

Kelly Owen

Any other day

I don't want to see Christmas
I want it to pass
I want it to gust through Winter
And fade in the past
I feel like the Grinch
I'm not welcoming Christmas
I'm not giving an inch
Or feeling that pinch
That pinch in the pocket
For that never worn bracelet
Or for that forgotten about locket
This year "Santa Clause lost it!"
But I'm in hibernation
Netflix at the ready
As I ignore the entire nation
Change the station
Half way through November
A Tinsel invasion…
It's crazy!
To be treated like any other day
With mash, pie and onion gravy!

Carol Sheppard

Apple

Saw a discarded apple on the pavement,
reminded me of you;
withered, bruised,
once a rosy beauty.
Teeth marks on your skin, chunks missing,
open wound to the core.
Should have picked you up,
placed you somewhere safe.
But I walked away,
let another git kick you in the gutter.

Akon Nouhry

A Prayer

Ô! I wish race were underpants
So discrete, intimate, scant
And justice the crown of a humanity
Fallen prey to malice and insanity.

Sue Finch

A Suitcase for Leaving
A new fairy tale for anyone who fancies a read...

For every child born,
a suitcase stored in the old woman's cupboard.
A peacock quill, dipped in stewed elder bark and sloe,
for each name tag.
On the kitchen table a wooden box;
carved into the lid a crow, silhouetted by a full moon.
Inside this box the cupboard's key.

It was said she knew the exact moment
each child would come to pick up their case
for their leaving journey.
Before gifting them their case
the old woman would bid each visitor to sit
for a hunk of bread,
a glass of red wine.

The day Silver arrived the old woman was surprised.
Her manners kicked in as she led her in,
Please sit down with me, she said
pointing to the second chair at the table,
Let us drink and have bread together.

Seven hundred thousand times before
she had poured wine,
but today as she turned for the loaf she frowned.
Here, have half, she said,
tearing a chunk in two.
Silver's hand paused;
in all the stories she knew
you ate the whole piece of bread.
But the old woman was already pulling her piece apart
stuffing it in her mouth.

Silver copied the chewing
drank wine to soften the crust in her mouth.
This was not what they said it would be like;
the bread was supposed to be warm from the oven,
its softness savoured slowly.
It was meant to be the kind of bread that had you
wanting more.

Glancing round the room
Silver's eyes noted the neat crosses
on the calendar on the old woman's wall.
A crossing through of days, a keeping of time.
But yesterday was not crossed through.

But it is my birthday, she thought,
this is the day I was born.
As she struggled to swallow the last crumbs
and find her voice
a dribble of wine ran down the glass onto the table.
You messy, ungrateful child, screamed the witch,
grabbing the girl by the throat with one hand
and tipping the key from the box with the other.

Too early, she muttered
as she stuffed Silver into the case
and fastened the zip.

Marilyn Timms

Autumnus: Roman Harvest Goddess

Fanfares are silenced now,
the harvest home;
the goddess, already half-forgotten,
is returning to the soil.
She carries the brown stench of decay,
of impending death.
Only her eyes are alive,
cradling the last of the sun.
Falling leaves whisper, This is not the end –
Remember her!

Laura Grevel

Ballad of Burg Rappotenstein

Up the Pehamsteig we pant through a forest does slant,
past grand dames of beech who dance on mossy limbs that peer askant,
to whisper our arrival to old Rapoto, Lord of Kuenring,
phantom who will decide which of eight gates
he allows us enter, or deny.
No matter that we beseech with speech!

My, now look there through the wood at one who was so very good:
Nepomuk strides in leathered hides, six-foot flintlock at his side,
hunting for hirsch, his Winter meat,
while the peasant Franz dogs his master's steps to eat.

We tiptoe now by granite boulders round like giants' heads—
they likely watch us in those chinks. I did, did you, see an eyelid blink?
Across the footbridge next a maple twin, ascending
high enough to see all sin,
we scramble like mischievous mice up and along a hoary oak's thighs,
scratched I'm sure by boys Heimo and Elmar as they snuck
to check their traps,
while birch steps a white-legged prance o'er shadowed trail
and pines twist rough-red up, up to grasp the light.

On! Near bright leavéd ferns to turn and sight the Burg
Rappotenstein's stolid might:
ancient towers and walls betray no lines, though deep grey larch
covers his time.
Does the Burg hold those granite cheeks and jowls,
or do those scowling igneous mounds hold it?

They allow us pass, these wanton walls that could easy crush
us with dislike
as they billow out in sails that fill on winds at lofty heights.
Yet, Ladies Gundula and Mechtild wave us enter

to one-after-yet-another gate and keep.
We gasp at elegant sgraffito window frames, and hornéd skulls
Of great cold beasts that adorn this intimate meeting feast.
There walks Ezechiel and Wolfram to greet their guest
King Ottokar of Bohemia.
He seeks their chest to ally against the Hapsburgs—oh what mut!—
To lend your hut on such a bold and brazen quest
that will send all to an exiles' lonely searching death.

Up we go to speak with Hieronymus who shows us frescoes
by Albin and Blasius, men well pleased to see their dainty
daily scenes not alarmed by rebel peasants, not torn by Catholic troops,
not scorned by stubborn Swedes, who three times tried
to ford this keep
and three times left widows who weep. And here is Walburga
to lead us to chapel,
where Konstantia and Apollonia do dapple the pews
with prayers of chattel.

And did you hear Hildegund call down the drafty passage
to küche beneath,
where roars a fire, heating soup of beef? And now hear neigh
the horses of Ottokar's entourage in full dressage,
who shout their cheer and Gott-Sei-Mit-Ihr,
that they have allies to tie to their hopes, to greet
an enemy's savage barrage.
Though forever in the dungeons rattle bones and bleak
that left their rot in icy sink
in the bowels of Rappo where aroma of soup and strength
doth not reach.

O Heimo and Elmar, you young men, rash and reckless without fear,
those rabbits cost dear, that you in traps on royal ground did set,
not thinking you'd be met, caught fast and hard in your own net.
And not even Una's pretty look, not Ida's secret smile and schmuck,
would weigh to help you out and clear from that deep dreaded
dungeon drear.

Because for six-hundred years the Graf von Abensberg und Traun
has drawn his liege from across this down and town.
And even from two-hundred years before, the weary geist of Burg,
old Lord Rapoto, steinig und stur,
would never let poor minions hunt his moor!

Matty Blades

Blood stain

Like burnt tears
Rolling down her cheeks
Blood-stained lips
That become too afraid to speak
Fear in her heart
The fear that she's forever tethered
Timid to the touch
Her nerve endings severed.

Tish Camp

Buildings (Haiku)

I painted the barn
in the last snow of your days
building memories.

Adele Ojier Jones

Circadian Riddle
This poem was written near the end of a northern winter, travelling to the southern hemisphere's autumn, unexpectedly caught in long lockdown, then back to the north for winter, with official permission to leave.

Three winters
either end of two summers
one autumn and spring
and now back to moonlight
well beyond seven,
even this, surely
beyond the realm of migrating birds
puzzling over the music
of circadian rhythm.

Back in the north
in the swing of things
bells in the dark
sounding through the valley
at midnight
reminding all that in this
a strange year to remember
celebrating
recalling family stories
is part of the rhythm.

Kuma San

Cocooned on warm sofa
I wrote this poem at a workshop with Josephine Lay.

Cocooned on warm sofa
fire hisses
wood sparks
licked by yellow flame
wind claws at windows
lashing water slides
down storm darkened glass
a candle flame stutters
spilling soft shadows
on dim walls
the tempest wails
I pull my blanket
up to my chin
warm
as I wriggle my toes.

Nick Lovell

Contact

You meet them once in a while.
People that you know
More in one shared crooked smile
than in others who have shared
many a mile and year.
They stand clear, somehow brighter
than others around,
shadows darker, colours lighter
Somehow more alive,
Movements sharper than the rest.
So much expressed, compressed
that one chance glance
into shared souls suggests
so many possibilities, alternative realities.
No boundaries to
our shared personalities here and now.
It isn't love or lust, though they can lie there,
It's deeper, purer.
It's an offer of trust, a connection, a spark
A mind-to-mind meeting, moonlight in the dark
but moments are too short
they slip by too fast,
Before either of you think to speak
the moment is passed
with a raised eyebrow or nod
Yet you both leave each other
with a memory that lasts.

Richard Adkins

Covid City
I walked about Gloucester on a wet, cold late February evening earlier this year. The idea was to paint pictures from words of a city brought low by the pandemic.

Darkness in the city
lost gaze of glowing sun.
Shuttered, quiet, broken now,
sirens, wind, paper trails.
Dying embers, life now gone
shielded, boarded, distant dreams.
Spires stand confused, neglect
seats, empty convent quiet kept.
Bells toll for life now gone, extinct
torn apart by quiet stealth of war.
Flags fly defiant, half-mast drawn
apologies on window frame
dulled by dirt; neglect and fear.
No Sundaes, waffles, pizza, cake
no chat, no joy, no time to meet,
Christmas tree stands sad and worn,
in February's battered gathering storm.
Bags, rags, mask a tumbleweed tear
Churches claim the 'Lord is near'.
Docks lie quiet, berths lay bare
gulls flutter, cry as in despair.
Water dark hides hidden depths
no food to eat no time to share.
No life is here but solitaire.

Gabby Wiest

Creature of the Night

The second time
I open my eyes
I feel something
that changes in me
I don't have
a heartbeat
I am cold like ice
I hear everything
around me
even the beat
of your heart.

I am thirsty
and your aroma
thrills me
your scent makes me
hungry even more
I become the hunter
of the night
my presence
makes you terrified
I feel your fear
that makes me smile.

Catrice Greer

Cygnus, Monogamous

Reference to Swans (female), mating and monogamy. Cygnus also pertains to "The Swann" - a northern constellation southwest of Draco, containing the bright star Deneb.

She goes by
as if skating on the pond
as if levitating
above the marsh city below
above the frogs, fish, worms
grassy fields swaying her on

Never matter
each day like the other
neck craned, mute
in her quiet watery solitude

uncoupled
there is only one
her feathers ivory
winged back
fluttering only slightly
a hint of a dream and desire
almost yawning
at the mundane

And there it comes
the last and only one
their foreheads touch single-hearted
entwined necks as growing vines

Coupled as one
boated at the helm
on the same course
a pairing to last for always.

Morgan 'I'm-not-a-poet' Rye

During a pandemic, in this economy

Send me to burn when I expire
No sniffing about my corpse
Just cut my wrists, make sure I'm dead
And tie me up in straw
Send me off in back of a truck
Don't wait to throw me in
My shell will not care at all
But my spirit will

May the gods of hail beat you raw
If the F-word is planned for me
Beechen rows that hurt your back
Fake velvet misery
May lighting strike you down
If you service in a room
May my gorgeous gods of thunder
Shake you from that gloom

Unlearn that death monstrosity
Commercial companies sell
Refute that awful yellow wood
And brass from compact slaves
Do not display a photo
Or mount a podium
Do not think that two of my songs
Will vibe a funeral on

Just wait until the box arrives
Or jug stuffed with a sock
Pick a day that suits you well
Bring music that you love
Into The New Forrest we will go
To make my journey day

Old the land my ancestors walked
There is where they wait

Lay blankets down for picnic
Or simply walk the woods
Know each other, smell the earth
Green, brown and blue
When the time is right, make a circle for me
Speak and let me go
Take care my pup, my little one
See her well from this day on.

Ian Paulin

Edge of dark and light

there is no middle only edge
each serrated wakening livens us
seek no sleep for comfortable centre
but bring a bleed to dawns we yearn

epiphany is a light that blinds
uncarves all shadows in a gleam
as we are bound to wreak oppression
deluge Damascus Road to free more souls

to the hear the Voice of calling
when I am at a depth that seems
beyond a climbing to redemption
help me sit among uncertain

oh, I am streaking to gate of heavens
and then to plunge beyond the suck of hell
and in this movement strides the freedom
in every beat that proves the death or Life

Kezzabelle Ambler

Emergency Muse

Let me wrap my words around you
soothe with syllables and TLC,
hold you safely in my prose
to heal today's life malady.

Where blunt harsh internal knocks
leave an eternal bruise,
let me ease the bully's disease,
let me be your rescue muse.

Let's soak hurting tears and fears
in calming psalms,
a devotional potion bathed daily,
a cleansing stanza balm.

Restful rhymes are
immunity remedies
that help alleviate
persistent anxieties.

Lullaby stitches applied carefully
to love lines torn apart,
turn time's pages with soft phrases
to mend a broken heart.

Sleepless nights and bad dreams
need a boost filled prescription,
playfully put right
with a comedic injection.

Calamities need anti-inflammatories,
to help all ills from getting worse,
ingested on a regular basis,
take a tonic via verse.

Sonnet power plasters
applied with poised fingers at the ready,
dulcet tones deliver poetic tomes
to keep life's balance steady.

Prayerful pen in hand,
no promise of heroics,
clauses formulated to serve,
I'm your emergency poet.

Darryl John

End

I hope you are all safe and well. I've been working on my Masters in not so sunny Salford and I'm growing my Instagram page for my poetry.

Black rain falls from the sky
burns the flesh, melts the brain,
faces drip blood like candle wax,

fuelled by greed
a need for power and control,
punished
Kosovo and Syria,
leukaemia and Aids
dirty bombs
and weapons
of mass destruction,

oceans once blue
now dyed black
fish float on the surface,
toxic clouds smother the air
the smell of decaying flesh,
nothing grows,
it's eerily quiet,
only shelter remains
underground

concrete bunkers for the rich
cancerous cells
for those left outside
cooked from within, organs failing,
the planet lies gasping
its air poisoned forever,
the black rain washes away
all traces of humanity

Alby Stockley

Fibroids

2 years since I knew my body
4 since I last felt comfort in it
There is a space grown
Between clots and bones
Where brittle tendons snap
Blue veins showcase translucent skin
Cysts and fibroids
Embrace my thickening womb
Increase and distort it's lining
Cause tidal flows
That fall with rushing warmth
Over and through towels and tampax
Run down my legs
Soaks through jeans
In public toilets I wipe
Blood and clots from my thighs
Check denim for stains
Sigh when it shows through
Amidst severe cramps and back pain
Swollen breasts that hurt to touch
In winter I remove my jumper
Tie it round my waist
To hide the red
That marks me unclean.

Gabby Wiest

Forbidden Love

Love is not mine
I am not qualified
to be loved by you
because I am
the wanderer
prohibited from
falling in love.

I belong to no one
not even you
can change
the will of heaven
I am a refugee of man
they adore me and love me
and leave me on the ground.

Chris Barber

From Intake to Uptake

Ain'tcha from our patch of dust?
Don'tcha think you're one of us?
Dunno why you ain't on our bus.
What's the point of all that fuss?

A drive to look and sound the same,
opportunistic politicos are to blame,
when you don't fit that fellowship frame,
or play the pointy finger game.

No, I don't think I'm better than you,
just different and we're not that few,
a real silent majority, those that do,
not the noise of hate and twisting truth.

So, I won't run with your pack,
or stand nervously shuffling at the back,
alone, free thinking, an alternative track,
trust in the Tribe I gladly lack.

Ann-Marie kurylak

Futile
5.00am poetry

I lie in the dark and look at the clock
Silent of its tick and tock
All the while hearing you move and turn
As the pain continues to burn
And you yearn for that sleep
But it escapes you
A sweet treat
That you can't keep
That takes you from our bed
Stealing away instead
I see you move away
Trying desperately to stay comfortable
But the pain is raw
And ragged
A deep sensation
Without cessation
A thief in your night
Tight and bright
I hear you sigh and I want to cry
As another night goes by
My efforts made futile
While you're robbed of rest
I've done my best
And yes, I've tried
To make the pain hide
But all for naught.
My love can only do so much
My touch though sweet
Cannot compete
Or defeat
My hugs tempered gentle
And censored by care
I wait and stare

At the ceiling and wonder
At my blunder
My failure to take it away
So that you will stay
In our bed.
I miss you there
My heart laid bare
To show you I care
Which is all I can dare.
So, I lie in the dark
And look at the clock,
You robbed of your sleep,
The clock of its tick and tock.

Keren Hermon

Government

The tomfools at the tiller
Cannot steer the boat
Feel confused by compass
Cannot swim or float

Don't look at the horizon
Misunderstand the maps
Don't know why cold wind blows
What storms are at their backs

If passengers get seasick
They are thrown overboard
No benefit of lifebelt
No kind supporting word

They struggle in the water
Most of them do drown
This pleases all the tomfools
It keeps expenses down.

DrayZera

Hexagonal Diagonal

Brain cells so Linear,
Clear like your flat fish.
A dish you serve daily,
Stop calling me daisy.
You cry, for lies.
You schemed, I screamed.
So, suck it, and pour the salt,
You cannot control me!
Brain cells so linear,
Clear like your flat fish.
Spare me the tissues,
You think that I miss you?
You cry, for lies.
You schemed, I screamed.
So, suck it, and pour the salt,
You cannot control me!
Hexagonal Diagonal,
Think you can control me.
Hexagonal Diagonal,
Think you can suppress me.
Hexagonal Diagonal,
Think you can depress me.
Hexagonal Diagonal,
Sugar honey. Iced bitch!

Keren Hermon

Hollow Man

Don't waste your spurious charm
on me Hollow Man.
I have seen you bare your teeth.
I know your pattern.
Your account of yourself,
as honest and caring,
has sprung very many leaks.
I think you soon will drown.
Your poisoned bait can't tempt
a newly lucid mind.
Control, coercion crumble.
Love was never present.
I see your shrivelled soul
struggle to survive.
Predator.

Becky Who

If you liked my poetry

If I could take the thoughts, you most like to think
And sculpt them into text that speaks to you as art,
If I could take the feelings, you most want to share
And mirror them in words, reflected in your heart,
Then would you more easily forgive my selfish pen?
Excuse the vacant looks, the lost half-hours when
I am not yours, a-wandering some distant mental shore.
If you liked my poetry, perhaps you'd love me more.

Derek Dohren

I Just Don't Know

Time's not linear
I lived a future life.
Event horizon whirlpool
now risking spaghettification.
When my cup of tea is finished
I'll go scale Hadrian's Wall again
with a bucket full of frogspawn
so, I can go and terraform Mars
in motionless friction.
The perfection of birdsong is noted
but I just don't know
if the space in my head
is habitable or inhabitable.

I'm annoying the neighbours
with a noisy kitchen blender.
I thought I'd thrown away
my only pair of scissors.
Just how do you decide
on a houseplant's gender?
Your honey sweet lips
and a laptop upon my knee.
I think I've matured with rage.
A photo of the family, minus me
but I just don't know
if the stuff of this world
is flammable or inflammable.

Steering wheel judder
hits at 45 miles per hour.
I didn't turn right into Monmouth
Instead, I turned a wrong.
Rainbow kissed flower

but damn those springtime blizzards.
I have lost all my perspective
and I'm waving at Vincent's wheatfield
a masterpiece of creation
spied through my shattered windshield
but I just don't know
if the experience of life
is valuable or invaluable.

Robert Lang

In-Crowd

I'm reading lots of comments across Social Media platforms, from people who are increasingly worried by new measures to curb the spread of COVID. Poetry can help I think, even if only in a small way, perhaps by raising others spirits. Here's a poem I cobbled together last March when the first lockdown came into force. If it lightens your mood a little, good enough! I hope it does.

In with the In-Crowd now!
Self-isolation can be a frustration
some feel it just isn't cricket
At least there's no doubt
who's in or who's out
as we've all got to stay
at the wicket
Keeping in touch matters ever so much
IT's really playing its part
A click here and there
a gregarious share
helps family & friends
to stay in good heart
Fresh air is good, you certainly should
take care to keep yourself fit
Walking's allowed
but not in a crowd
please keep in mind
the government's writ
Good news at least is in from the east
a decrease in released CO_2
The air in Wuhan is
now cleaner than Cannes
and they'd only one case in
the last day or two
Think also on this with so much so amiss
while wrinkling a fevered brow

Stuck there at home
you're not on your own
you're well in with
the In-Crowd now!

Devlin Wilson

I see you

I survey you from the crow's nest
Of an island-hopping tramp steamer
Becalmed amongst the dregs
Of three continents

I observe you from the control tower
Of an abandoned aerodrome
Risen above the flotsam and jetsam
Of failed prototypes

I monitor you from the battle deck
Of a beached landing craft
Drifting in an elephant's graveyard
Of midget submarines

I glimpse you furtively through
A chink in your bedroom curtains
Your body eerily backlit
By night vision ultraviolet.

I see you.

Scott Cowley

It's a lonely life
Sat in kitchen, Tom Robinson on 6music. And me… typing and drinking

a good friend of mine recently
said these following words to me
"You are an artist and a poet,
it's a lonely life my friend"
so, I'll raise the bottle (fuck the glass)
and say cheers
for the words that follow these…

it's the witching hours, the three-a.m.'s
then the over thinking takes over
and over and over, and
reality kicks in
you'll be drinking coffee
in the morning alone again
with a broken envelope
and a half blunt pencil in hand

the drinking coffee turns into
necking down the half empty bottle
on the kitchen worktop
it's just less of an inconvenience
than washing out a dirty mug which
has been sink-sitting for days
easier than kettle-switch flicking

ah yes, that switch
you know the one, the nagging itch
constantly being hassled to
finish that commission piece
it's certainly not been just weeks
it's been months, but no drama
I'll have it finished next Tuesday!

so, the coffee never made it
to the sink sodden mug
the next bottle got throttled
and its innards "chugged"
like any good alcoholic poet would
with a half blunt pencil and
the back of a broken envelope

picking up phone with the vaguest ideas
of actually logging into Facebook
semi socially interacting for a
fraction of time well spent doing something else

picks up phone, writes text explaining
to those who've been patiently waiting
you can't rush good art (with no apology)
that there above line will
make up part of my eulogy?
well, it better do or I'll come back and
haunt the fuck out of you! (with no apology)

it's the witching hours, the three-a.m.'s
and with the grace of God
all being well
you've been here before and
you'll be here head scratching again
the tick of the clock tormenting

I know I've made promises
stood behind the mic and
bared my soul for all to see
tattooed words, ink upon me

picks up bottle, writes text explaining
I'm a functioning alcoholic
so please be patient.
your inbox will be receiving

at some point next Tuesday a piece
of greatness, a classic for your reading

I'll not make promises
last time around was
a different kind of pain
I'll be able to shift this but
like I say "no promises"
and maybe there'll be no cliff?

remember where this all started
one functioning alcoholic to another
man, I'd gladly slit palm, make brother
and we'll get back to a point, where
I'll dredge sink-sodden mugs
where we can sit in a place
and share a mug of tea again
with the caveat of no promises, my friend

I'd like to finish off
one of my greatest hits
admittedly half pissed
as my normality currently is
with pencil in one hand
and sobriety in white knuckled fist

"You are an artist and a poet,
it's a lonely life my friend"

Darcy Royce

Jennie in a Bottle

You're pellucid to me, darling,
Nabokovian,
in places, others cannot reach,
or is it the touch,
that renders your heart lustrous,
and your extasy,
this prolonged,
this songful,
and high pitched?

Chthonic, I follow in your mazes,
unornamented,
tenebrous wolf to your manner,
seraphic woman
for the taking,
I'm barely lucid,
at that one last thrust,
and small death,
of angels, love, and dagger.

Franchesa Kirkpatrick

Leaving Darkness in Pine Trees Burning

Darkness reminds me of Winter.
Smells of pine trees burning from Christmas.
Gatherings to play music in celebration of memories.
Focus on what you want to bring into the light.
Leave the dark on bits of paper burning in the night.

Ann D Stevenson

Lockdown

Information, education
on the present situation.

Intimidation,
pontification:
stay in location,
no integration,
no vacation,
no celebration,
just segregation,
and separation.

For stimulation
and inspiration
use imagination,
conversation,
communication.

Until medication,
for rehabilitation,
despite deprivation,
desperation, irritation,
frustration
and temptation,

avoid dissemination,
annihilation,
obliteration and damnation,
show consideration,
no procrastination,
stay in isolation,
Save The Nation.

P.S. Jubilation,
a vaccination,
major celebration!

Jason Conway

Melness Sunset

The pilled cooling land gently slopes and rises like a freshly aired linen sheet, rippled across an endless cushioned bed

Shimmering white rocks break the undulating curves of a brocaded heath, buttoned by fluffed Cotton Grass tufts

Sponge like mounds of moss, clover and heather spring inquisitive wanderers, like giants hopping across islands

Stroking winds make grass roll, tidal like, sending silvery snakes to wind towards the hem of glowing hills

Sunset draws down a violet damask drape to peach and lemon folds that snug a rusted aubergine pillowed landscape

Not long now, for the circling sun to rest beneath the rich lustrous fabric of the moon's speckled sequin quilt

This ever-giving Celtic land, tucked by the brush of the North Sea, is a waking dream of the wild and will always lie with me.

Valerie Hartill

My Darling

My Mum wrote a poem about loss. I think it was written about 3 months after she was widowed. I was shown it today....it struck me as a beautiful note on grief. She is happy to share it so I thought here would be the best place. X Kuma San

They who are near me,
do not know that you are nearer to me than they are.
They who speak to me,
do not know that my heart is full with your unspoken words.
They who crowd my path,
do not know that I am walking alone with you.

Nick Lovell

My Generation
First draft of something daft.

It's the retirement home of the future, once the boomers have all died
But don't expect grey hair and tweed if you venture on inside.
There's fashion sense and dyed hair, Mohicans, skins and dreads
Coz we might be knocking on a bit but we ain't the living dead.

We're not the sort for a tea dance, you gotta understand.
We want DJs, MCs, Dealers. We want a proper hard rock band.
We might be old but our hearts are young, we were generation X,
We want what's left to be like the past, full of booze and drugs and sex.

There'll be orgies in the day lounge, cocaine lines across the table.
Three Grandad gimps in the corner, down on their knees in front of Mabel.
And the sex swing comes in real handy, for those who've had a hip op
The whole scene set to the sweet sound of some dirty 90s hip hop

We're banned from having Mandy, our own fault I must confess.
The staff say it makes us too randy and they can't cope with all the mess.
And the matrons had a breakdown, it simply all became too much
After a midnight call to Mr West to remove a hover tube from his crotch

We used to go out skinny dipping on a nice warm summer's night
Till the sight of naked bodies in the gloom gave the sea scouts such a fright
When relatives come to visit, we are good and nice and proper
Can't even have a crafty spliff coz old David's son's a copper.

We grow weed out in the greenhouse, we brew poteen in the shed,
We make the most of the time we've left, coz I's fucking long time dead.
So come join our wild fiesta, *do not go gentle into* that dark night.

We'll drink and laugh and dance away till our very last twilight.

Because I have seen the grim alternative, dying slowly, inch by inch,
Bereft of joy, beset by pain, that's a fate from which I flinch.
They say that the important thing is to age with dignity,
Well, that might be alright for some, but it is not the way for me.

Gemma Crow

My ripples, My pond
Feeling brave enough to share after attending last nights 'Crafty Crows' zoom event. Felt great to reconnect and hear wonderful poetry again.

Ghostly prejudice dances through,
I watch it with my inner eye,
Appreciate its origin and respect its warning.
I can't control the ghosts that cavort through,
My ancestor's shadows casting their doubt.
I do control the response I have to those shifting shapes,
Whether to feed them with my own darkness.
I decide whether I drown them with light, banish
them to seep out of sight.
I decide on my response, my thoughts are not guilty,
my actions could be.
I challenge myself daily, especially now.
Have I exorcized the entities that so freely float?
Or are they haunting my interactions?
From my vantage point can I even judge?   Who can?
So pushed into silence, I close myself in,
The light diluted letting shadows creep in.
Ancestors louder, bolder, fiercer,
Compounding, affirming, giving credence to fears.

Chloë Jacquet

My Sofa is Missing You

She's been crying
sofa tears,
which means dust and fluff everywhere
and I'm not managing to
keep on top of the cleaning.

The pillows on your side of the bed
are missing you.
I can hear them sighing
while I dream.
Their sorrow
has given them that yellow tinge
I discover when I undress
them of their cases.

Your favourite pint glass
with the handle
from that beer festival
is missing you.
He pines for your lips,
your thirsty sips.
His tears leave drip marks
outlined in salty white
even after his fairy liquid bath.

Polly Stratton

My stalwart friend
This poem is for Patricia Camp who, despite year upon year of accumulated trauma, still shows up for herself and others.

They beam ego and self, through your "translucent" skin
They take residence reside within
You run, fetch
Give
Grieve
Make connections
Forged with courage
Make excuses
Make the bed
Again.

Viva O'Flynn

New Life

look not so sullen
when you see me gone
sunny skies and smiles
still dance before your eyes
earthy soil blooms into new life
spurts promises and eases strife
sombre black never suited your style
glow like a rainbow does in exile
after the storm clears shake off your fears
leave yesterday's episode
unpack your load
winds of change blow directions unknown
as a sweet soft sigh carries me home.

Clive Oseman

Not in my Name

There are some people I want to mention tonight
Whose tragic deaths magnify the need
to fight for equal rights
rise up and shout "Enough is enough,
this is not in my name."

I want to mention:
Jamar Clark, Philando Castile,
Breonna Taylor, Botham Jean.
These people are a small proportion
of those who are gone,
lost to racism and hatred
black lives ended in the United States,
and still the toll increases.

Sean Reed, Ahmaud Arbery,
Michael Brown, Ezell Ford.

You could add to this list of course
because it's a shameful rollcall
of lives that mattered,
with loved ones whose lives were shattered.
Their names are scattered
through the mists of time
and this list of mine, is just a sample,
a small example of racist crime
and institutional homicide.

Michelle Shirley, Trayvon Martin
Kenny Watkins, Tamir Rice, just twelve years old.
So many tragedies to be told.
Eric Garner, Tony McDade.
Anyone can add more names.

George Floyd.
His death sparked protests worldwide
which in the States were met with force,
encouraged by a president in too deep with the KKK,
who then had the nerve to say,
how George could "look down on a great day
a great thing that's happening for our country."

And you think it's just in America?

There are some people I want to mention tonight
whose deaths magnify the need
to fight for equal rights
rise up and shout "Enough is enough,
this is not in my name."

I want to mention:
Sean Rigg, Mikey Powell, Mark Duggan.
Lives lost in the United Kingdom.
You probably know of others.
People who were sons, daughters,
Fathers, mothers. The list is long.

Leon Briggs, Ricky Bishop,
Stephen Lawrence, Joy Gardner.

We have to resist, try harder.
Raise awareness, demand respect and fairness
regardless of the colour of a person's skin.
If you stay silent, you're aiding and abetting.

And please, save your indignant
"All lives matter"
Your ignorant dismissal of white privilege
your claims that this campaign makes you a victim.

Because all lives do matter, not just yours,
including those throttled by a copper's knee
as they lie helpless on the floor.

Now if that were routine for the likes of you
what do you think you would do?

Tish Camp

Nubian Queen
Jeanette Ade Osunsanya - 11th March 1986 - my darling sister

You begin in the title of a book
protector and Black Panther
you roam across wastelands
of Elephant and Castle
defied monsters there
and beat down doors

you were natural, fierce
even with freckles
and had philosophies
spill like petals from your lips
your books, jewels
knowledge of kings
beset in the crown
of a Nubian Queen.

Othello is your moreish Moor
on your sunken velvet horsehair chair
leg skin preened and oil
shinning stage, lights on each
every hair sat firmly
like your seat, in pores

my pride at your mouth, open
eyes widen at pupil's core
absorbing his hand-neck drama
Desdemona death
and tears in mine at hers

and yours

the rope, imagined scarf
upon your neck

a story-lie of flight in winds
the stage - the act - the scene.

Black skin, freckle count on face
I recant like desert sand
through fingers of disbelief
into time returned
of love for a Nubian Queen
Black Panther
sister, sleep.

Lacey Tidwell

Numbers Are Up, So I'm Back In Covid ICU

This was taken from a Facebook entry by Lacey, reposted by one of my friends. It was originally posted in prose, almost in the form of a letter from a nurse to her patient. The words and story flowed through the piece with some beauty, so much so, that I thought it might deserve an attempt at capturing it as a poem. Only the format has been changed.
Trevor Valentine.

To my patient I had last night
I reviewed your chart before I greeted you
And knew we had a battle ahead of us

You asked me when I walked in
"Do people on this machine make it out of here alive?"

I knew you were scared

So was I

You fought through the night
And I watched your monitor closely
Cheering internally
Each time I saw your oxygen trending up

However, there came a time
Early in the morning
Where you stopped trending up
Your alarms continued through the unit
Without pause

You were dying

I geared up
And knew what was coming
But you had no idea
I walked in your room

And stood by your side

You were breathing too fast for oxygen to get to your lungs
And no amount of medication was helping

Your alarms continued

So now the doctor is in your room
And, believe it or not, he's scared too
You're very sick, and we need to do something fast

He finally breaks the news to you
Your lungs are too sick
And you need to be sedated
Paralysed
Placed on a ventilator
And turned on your belly
So, you can breathe better

This is what you were afraid of
This is what you told me scared you the most
Because you heard people
Who are placed on ventilators
Don't make it

I held your hand and told you
"Look at me, eyes on me
Don't worry about these alarms
Let us worry about those
Right now, it's you and me
I've been here all night
and I'll continue to be here for you."

You looked at me with tears in your eyes
Squeezed my hand, and then it was time

After a few seconds you were sedated and paralysed
We put your breathing tube in

But the alarms continued

It took 3+ hours of being in your room by your side
Your alarms stopped

For now, you're finally stable

So, to my patient
I gave you life-sustaining blood pressure medication
So, your organs didn't die
I gave you sedation so that you weren't in pain
I gave you paralytics so your lungs could rest
And the machine could do the work for you
But now I'm giving you prayers

Please fight
Because I'm fighting for you.

Kelly Owen

One very fucked up "I love you!"

This is my shouting poem
I'm Kelly Owen
Insist you definitely love me
But hey you're going?
Straight to your ex's
After almost two weeks of silence
Would have affected me less
If you'd had kicked out with violence
But I got silence!
No wanting to sort things out
I wanted you to shout
Find out what this really is about?
You gave me that doubt
I get ill and you disappear
It's ok "You still love me"
"Hello… Where the fuck are you dear?"
That's why I don't believe you love me
Shit gets real… you leave me be?!
You ran straight to be with your ex?
You even moved in until I went?
After your mother offered you a bed?
But you love me…
If four times running is love?
You're not right in the head!

Marilyn Timms

On Hold

Remission is such a dull word.
It lies limply on the tongue
a slow-puncture word,
hissing motes of meaning
by apologetic, imperceptible degrees
to pinch and prick my understanding
before settling softly and silently
like flakes in a snow-globe –
a total anti-climax.
I craft a den of duvet and pillows
burrow into the unfamiliar luxury of sleep;
marching bands and fireworks can wait.

Sue Finch

Overnight

You have changed the font
of all the funeral parlour names
to comic sans.

You have taken every lightbulb
from the amber of the traffic lights.

You have abandoned wet, black cardigans
in the middle of roads
to be dead black cats
catching my eye
before the sun splits the sky in two.

You have made all Autumn leaves
still clinging to the trees
only sour yellow.

You have torn each dropped leaf.

You have left me one small, dead cat
where I slow for the final roundabout.
A momentary discarded cardigan;
its body curled as if sleeping.

Charlie Markwick

Paroles de Joie

The aging radiance of the winter sun
long shadow patterns on the grass
the village tocsin warns
that dusk is waiting in the wings.

I set my chair way off the house
to catch the sustenance of light.
Silhouetted by the sheer
and darkening blue sky
the barn with roman tiles
the oak with ancient darkened boughs.
The chilling air is full of subtle sounds,
pigeons burbling, distant barking dogs
Jeanneau locking up the chickens
for the night.

The chill is playing round me now
no discomfort just a prod
that eventide is on its way.
I sip my beer
revel in contented thoughts
relishing the gifts, I've found in life.

Tournous-Darré – 03/01/21

Isobel May

Peace

Picked up a pen for the first time in years yesterday. Here is a first (very first!) draft of this piece.

I stand naked,
There is no hatred.
It's respite from anguish - ceasefire.
This peace is a truce within me
An alliance between head
and heart
body and mind
just
in time.

Cause I'm mates with my soul again.
Fuck,
I love her to pieces.

Death can wait.

No longer killing time
but birthing moments.
It's easy to let go cause
the pieces they fit different, now.

See the devil was always in the details.
And I don't pick apart
the pieces in my head, now.
The only voice in my head
is mine
now.
Peace
and quiet.

But peace doesn't have to be quiet.
You don't have to paint

your piece by numbers.
Be your own peacekeeper and let the world
know.
Let the world see
you.
Stay
whole.

Carol Sheppard

Phone Box

The phone box stands on the street corner
red paint peeling, faded in the sun,
ivy fingers creep across misted windows
'Carl was 'ere' scratched with a penknife,
'Daisy loves Jake' penned on the wall.
A dog sniffs at the door, cocks a leg;
later the drunks from the pub will piss inside.
The handset swings like an empty noose
waiting to ring but no one calls any more.

Jonathan Robert Muirhead

Poem – Preacher – Draft 1

The sign I see, dripping
With the moisture of rain
And perhaps also tears
Outside of the church
Somehow, a virginal white
Discoloured by time, temperance
And, above all, by man
Passing by every day
Yet still, it's here
There will be no
Act of public worship
Here today - and yet
There are plenty that
I can see in
The streets all around,
Life being breathed slowly
Back into a city
Which has rhythm in
It's bones and acid
On its tongue as
It laughs in defiance
And agrees in sympathy
With the world and
The situation it's in
Yet still, the sign
Stares back at me
From outside a church
That hasn't heard voices
Of Christians for months
Yet feels their souls
And feeds their minds
Every day, I smile
And I walk on

Again, as around me
I see young lovers
Kissing with abandon and
Children playing with parents
All in different mindsets
All here and yet
In their own worlds
A foot in each
A heart in both
The sign still stands
Ignored by all but me
And I smile as
I think just how
Both sets give
The lie to it.

Becky Who

Poetic Warning

WARNING
This world is under poetic surveillance
The POETS are watching

No image, sound or experience is guaranteed safe
from being found… inspiring

They will take feelings you didn't know you had
and turn them into words you didn't know you needed

They may not know who they are
but once they get started
they can be unstoppable
and unforgettable.

And REMEMBER
There could
Right now
Be a poet hiding
Inside

YOU.

Gemma Crow

'Potential too alluring'

Hello! It's been a while so hope you are all keeping well!
I thought I would share a poem about my endeavours with ink!

Wet ideas transform
Before hopeful eyes
Evaporating questions
Asked from the soul
Negative spaces
Shaping the answers
Tangled hues losing identity
Unfamiliar alliances form
Darkened edges yet to define
Intellect begs intervention
The artist patiently waits
Muddied eyes translate
The illusive spark
Yet to catch
Imagination not quite captured
Repeat.

Matty Blades

Rare Marble

Are you there my sweet?
Can you hear these words?
I shout them from the roof top
Hoping that they'll be heard

I wish you could talk to me
It's been so long since I heard your voice
Even when you were shouting
Your tone was so beautifully poised

I wish you could see me now
Standing tall upon my feet
No longer begging for change
After surviving so long on the street

I so hope that you'd be proud of me
For the man that I've become
I try every day in making strides
To become a better man

I remember the day you saved me
From trying to end it all
Telling me that you loved me
Laying the razor to the floor

You were a rare blue marble
As you meant the world to me
Still to this day, I can't understand
Why it is that God set you free

Maybe heaven needed another angel
Perfect you would be
Reaching out to other lost souls
As you once did for me.

Marilyn Timms

Realisation

Tonight, cancer,
I see your true colours:
sour yellow with shadows
of greenish-purple pulsing
underneath your skin.
You are a toad-shaped moraine
left by a retreating glacier
stoppering my life. A pirate.
You smell of stagnant ponds,
old churches, chicken innards.
Your voice is the hiss of willow
branches flayed by the rain,
floating on the wind
like a young girl's hair.
Never again, you whisper.
Everything is finished!

Tom Cooke

Salmonella Sid Stoker and Chef

Salmonella Sid was Chief in the Mess
Though where he was trained was anyone's guess
Some thought he'd served on a frigate or two
As when he ladled the food to the front of the queue
The bloke at the back always got some of your nosh
As Sid swayed to and fro, he was always sloshed
Now nobody ever dared criticise Sid
No matter what your rank or how bad the food
Cos Sid was definitely one of a kind
And in each meal that he served; you'd never guess what you'd find
He specialised in pies with thick pastry and sauce
Though what should have been beef
Could have been hedgehog or horse
A stoker he'd been at some time in his life
Which is probably why he'd not found a wife
His family were the blokes of the crew
Who he'd cuss and swear at if they wouldn't eat his stew
And to him the First Mate didn't stand on the deck
It was a huge fat seagull with a flexible neck
Who'd sit on the window edge where he was first served
Fed on the finest as Sid said it's what he deserved
As he and the seagull were one of a kind
Both were as free as the wind and independent of mind
Where Sid and the seagull are, is anyone's guess
In the name of progress, they tore down the mess
They replaced hard oak benches with tables and chairs
So no longer in lines we all sat in pairs
The banter was gone, deemed politically incorrect
And when the Number One called by, he got far less respect
Than Sid, the chief did, who now calls from the grave,
"You'll eat what you get, now sit down and eat what yer gave."

Clive Oseman

Shakespeare in the Age of Doom and Zoom
So, a newcomer to Shakespeare watched a Zoom discussion and was inspired to write some poetry based on the quotes he heard. Unfortunately, the connection was very poor and he got it terribly wrong... The first few lines are the first words spoken by Antonio in Merchant of Venice. It rapidly accelerates downhill from there...

In sooth I know not why I am so sad.
It wearies me, you say it wearies you;
But how I caught it, found it or came by it,
what stuff 'tis made of, whereof it is born,
I am yet to learn.

Come on mate. You caught it at Asda
from a fabbing, flap-mouthed foot-licker,
who went sans mask to buy his liquor!

All the world's a plague
and all the 5G masts are covid spreaders.
We wear our masks, and social distance
and those so inclined sayeth their prayers,
but should we cough or sneeze or such
we attract such hateful, anxious glares,
the suspicion all becomes too much -
in a web of fear, we are ensnared.

The holiday in Jersey is not strange,
'tis relatively covid free.
I much prefer to go to Spain,
but verily fuck that quarantine.
If you must holiday in England
go to the coast, don't stay inland
with grimy cities and, forsooth, its towns
like shitty Warwick bringeth frowns.

Alas, poor Warwick, its sewers smell
so putrid as to make one heave.
Within five miles I feel unwell
and the locals beg to take their leave.
Anne Hathaway once travelled that way
to meet a man with famed virility
but his breath smelt of shit and he wore a toupee
so, she ended up with me.

Wow is the winter in our discount tent
purchased in the Argos sale.
It was flimsy and weak, just upped and went
leaving us bare in a howling gale.
Shylock wanted his pound of flesh
Antonio went pale
Bassanio stole a beautiful Porsche
but the pigs let him out on bail.

All your sisters have got old.
and so have you-
You pribbling weather bitten haggard.
You think you look youthful, but truth be told
your flesh, it teems with maggots.

Now I'll try to keep this bit brief
because it's all it doth befit,
and after all, 'tis my belief
That brevity is the HOLY SHIT!!!

Hath not I got blue eyes?
Have not I got blue hands,
and a blue, err… ORGAN?
Fucking hell. Call an apothecary.

THE QUOTES I MANGLED *(For anyone who knows as little Shakespeare as I actually did before I researched this piece, and still do really)*

"All the world's a stage, and all the men and women merely players"
"The quality of mercy is not strained"
"Alas, Poor Yorrick. I knew him well."
"Now is the winter of our discontent"
Portia is a beautiful heiress who marries Bassanio against her father's wishes in the Merchant of Venice. And of course, despite the fact that I never say it properly, Porsche is pronounced like Portia.
"All that glisters is not gold"
"Brevity is the soul of wit"
"Hath not a Jew eyes, hath not a Jew hands, organs....."

'fabbing flap-mouthed footlicker'
'pribbling weather bitten haggard.'

Are phrases I got using a "Shakespeare insult generator" online. They are all words actually used by Shakespeare, but not necessarily together in the same insults!

DrayZera

Shapeshifters Lullaby
Three decades living in this world.
So much to grasp still in this world.

Three decades of this battered body,
Misunderstood by everybody.
I want to be somebody,
Yet I am nobody.
Shaping this future is difficult,
Sanding the rough - edge of this rock, I'm miserable.
I don't know where to turn; forever unstable,
As this body is burdened by labels.
Cut tension with a knife as light fades,
I wish this shapeshifter of mine would find grace,
As I want my malignant side to lose face.
I got my eyes down my iron sights.
As time makes use of my tired eyes.
And I have felt lost my entire life,
Now the hourglass is running out
And the sand is running down.
And the rain is pouring now,
And no longer I am loud.
No longer I'm allowed,
No longer I'm allowed,
No longer am I proud...
No longer am I a shapeshifter,
No longer... I'm a shapeshifter.

Sue Finch

Silence

Silence stands in the hallway all night
says she doesn't need to sleep.
In the morning she is in the chair
waiting.
Sometimes she smiles
and I think she gave me the dream
about meeting Dolly Parton for the soundcheck.
Sometimes she is so aloof
I imagine she sent me the handless mob
lumbering towards me,
bloodied boxing gloves
where fingers should have been.
She has birdsong in her;
sends the call of a bittern
to make me laugh
after she has taken me to the darkest silence.
Once she tapped me on the shoulder
at 3am, handed me the car keys
got in the car with me
and directed me to a forest.
She took me over a stile
to the darkened path
where we could not see our feet
and the bumps and gnarls of roots
sat under the mud.
Before my eyes adjusted
she stopped me
stood with me
to hear the last owl
and the first blackbird.
Once she wrote me a note
folded it and put my name on it
so she could watch me open it

and read.
I am your shadow, it said
in a spidery hand.
Her drawings tattooed the page –
a tarnished axe,
a coffin,
and a holly bush,
all its leaves on the ground.

Previously published by 'One Hand Clapping' in September 2020

Tish Camp

Slept in My Dress

I slept in my dress -
champagne and sparkles, the cause
eyelashes stuck on, applying catholic guilt like paint
to the sore head bed
lips pink outlined in six a.m. sun

in my blue moon - corking pop
and cracking fun
heading for stars, bright galaxies
are hidden by black hole
swallow, swallowed swig
dress - love - shift

a comet with burning tail
captivate - lash - expire
meteoric storm, raining glitter
in lurex, spandex subtext
I am stretched

pulled across perfumed skin
Lady Million Paco Rabanne, for him
fitting, cling, heady,
open neck - the space - aromas rise
towards his imagined mouth
there he devours dandelion wish
girl with the dragon tattoo on shoulder - breathes her spoken fire

drunken shame pressed into pillow
create crease - she is sunk
like solar ship
with trashy space cargo
dress mess - taut on thigh
tight - tease - tripping
in hungover sky.

Kezzabelle Ambler

Spellings

A dark cauldron full of thoughts and words,
past and present, lost and found.
Shredded inks link adjectives,
tasty verbs sprinkled with grated nouns.
Pint of hope stirred in
with a fountain pen of youth,
feelings of unrest,
forgotten font memories – twist of truth.
Beating hearts of green princes,
aye of fresh new beginnings.
Pinch of path-crossing stories
mixed together - life spell innings.

Carol Sheppard

Step forward to the new year...

Leave footprints
Don't look back
Let the trees whisper behind you
And the wind swirl and bite
Your footprints will fade
Leave the year behind

Devlin Wilson

Sunday with the Dead

The reading rooms remain padlocked
Bolted and shuttered, exhaling
The fungal miasma of bookish decay.
Corridors piled with motheaten tomes,
Eulogies, elegies and epistles,
Weather-warped and broken-spined
Tinder for the brackish trail of smoke
Rising from the crematorium of words.
Admittance is by luncheon voucher only;
A dank and dusty welcome for
The timeworn shufflers who queue here
To pass another mournful Sunday,
A becalmed and brooding Sunday
With the dead.

Once a solitary white stallion
Imposed order upon thousands;
The hoof prints of authority sounded
A drumbeat across the sacred topsoil
As packed stadia rocked to glory, glory days.
Now the stands sit empty
Bereft of rattle, scarf and klaxon
No massed choirs or mass support
To besmirch the quiet of the grave.
An ageing pundit grapples with
Fitful memories of Eusebio.
Having to face another Sunday,
This unathletic Sunday
With the dead.

Household gods tented by dust-sheets;
Obscure totems dimly revealed
By the light from tarnished globes.

Moon hollowed doorways
Exude aniseed and amaryllis.
Vanquished proprieties linger
Like the upright posture decreed
By a whalebone exoskeleton.
Echoes of musical soirees
Drifting through landscaped gardens
Greet the restive spirits who gather
To spend another listless Sunday,
One more benighted Sunday
With the dead.

Brian Reid

Sunrise on Cherhill
First positive piece in 6 months!

The night was still in its pomp as we rose.
Darkness illuminated by a huge, low Moon.
Sleep still tugged at me as I quaffed a banana shake
and thought about the coming day.
Fear grips in so many ways, all painful and unexpressed
But opportunity bests anxiety and I am focussed
on the moving parts of our endeavour.
The Plan
The People
The Philosophy
The Energy
The Excitement
The Expectation
Parked in a dawn struck layby before the climb.
The light is enough to recognise how steep and long
our track must be.
My only goal is reaching the top before the Sun breaks
on the horizon.
No words, just laboured breathing and the screams of thighs
buttocks and lower back.
Eyes front, head lowered into the storm of gravity
Ignoring the efforts of my younger, more agile colleagues
whose youth and fitness, leaves me embarrassed.
But my pace is steady and focussed.
No exasperated outbursts or impassable features
Slowly but surely making my way with only the Sun to beat
Suddenly the obelisk towers above me and my Compadres
wave and holler thru the dawn chorus.
The winds scythe across the summit
Biting unfettered through the layers, my cheeks reddened
through effort and exposure.

We are here and waiting for the chink of light
that heralds the new day.
We set up and shoot take after take.

Measuring, framing, working together, staying in the moment
and listening hard.
No dialogue but so many signals, thoughts, hopes,
mind's eye replays and channelling the spirit.

The Sun advances like a messenger of God a speck becoming
a dazzling crescendo of limitless energy but still and dreamlike
as our energy soars and we wrap the location shots
and head downhill.
Back to the world, full of people, streets and traffic,
all set for the daily bustling activities which mark
every Saturday morning.

Jason Conway

Tape my mouth
This is written for those that have been silenced and oppressed and those that are being stripped of their rights to peaceful protest.

Tape my mouth and
bind my hands,
string me up in
public execution.

A prowling pack stalks, growling,
hungry from the scent of
scapegoats, baited for
rows of toothed gallows,
spitting blood in closure.

The spectacle is staged,
carefully orchestrated by
defensive lions
fiercely protecting
their shrinking, royal reign.
They mark their stale territory
with the stench of history,
a golden rage of
savagery and feasting,
across open borders
to prey upon fresh meat,
expand their boundaries,
claw their legacy
and lick their spoils with pride.

Tape my hands and
bind my mouth
hang me by a string
as opinion swings.

Wrinkled elephants thud dry soil;
old memories stirred,
tall tales celebrated
of crushed opposition by the
sheer hulk of their imposing world.

An unstoppable stampede
trampling sacred ground,
syphoning watering holes
and revelling in rich mud,
bathing its wealth,
the fat of other's land.
You left dust clouds for
thirsting mouths,
boneyards for those charged
in your wake,
for the sake of your intentional,
unquenchable taste,
steered by raging bulls
embracing their impact
in displays of maddened power.

You tape my mouth and
bind my hands,
string me up for
public retribution but

my voice, all our voices
will be heard
above the compliant herd
and our determined fists
will punch the clouded sky.

We have the right to defy
our historical suppression,
demonstrate that right
to stir a deafening roar,

an uncomfortable fuss
to demand a public confession
of calculated oppression,
systematically imposed
by big cats and the giant
shakers and movers
that built their futures
with forced entry
and mauled tradition,
an empire of blood and bribes,
suspicion and convenient lies.

No, we will not be tamed and
you will not have our trust,
no matter how hard
you try to silence us.

Josephine Lay

The Abscission of Trees
(first draft)
'Abscission'. I only recently learnt what it means; it's the process by which the tree slowly cuts off the supply of sap to the leaves.

Deep in the deciduous forest
listen to the singing of leaves
as Death clothes
them in the raiment of Kings.

Here is no grim reaper
scythe in hand.

See him dance between the trees
his golden cloak flying
his feet scattering the fallen leaves.

This then is the zenith of life,
this moment of dying.

Praise the wrinkling of skin
the dulling of eye
the whitening of hair.

Learn to fall gracefully
gilded by the folds of his cloak.

Morgan 'I'm-not-a-poet' Rye

The boards are bare,

Like her salad box
And pension pot
And face where only skin and wrinkles stay.
The heating does not heat.
Adequate, the professionals say
Plumes of vapour sky her bedroom
To ice a single, ill-fitting glaze.
Walls are soft with damp and age
Paint falls in tiny flakes like snow
Onto the boards, between the cracks
Where legged fish and spiders live.
Fingers sting with cold
Stitching silks, to velvet, to cottons from the east
Things she collected and saved
Just in case.
Small pieces grow to fold and drape
Fringed and trimmed with weight
In rapture of a life lived
They layer her bed.
In that cold and damp room
In that adequate space
Her fingers bleed under the thaw
Of a beautiful place to sleep.

Trevor Valentine

Josephine ran a wonderful poetry workshop, to help all us budding poets. A Winter Warmer Workshop, first one of four. Josephine took us through incremental stages of developing and introducing different aspects into a poem, firstly a simple paradox or contrast between two experiences or thoughts. And then adding different elements, such as disturbances. It really can be quite surprising what you can lock away in your subconscious.

The Broken Chord

I look for the perfect chord
But find dissonance instead
An arpeggio partially sounding
The broken chord
But sweeter in its isolation
It finds its own harmony
Outside the structure of a key
It is there and always has been
Hiding and yet free.

Trevor Valentine

The Dandelion Poem
For Michael

Imagine for one moment
A dandelion seed head
Perfectly formed
And I purse my lips
And blow
Blow it out
To the four winds
And the seven seas
And by some miracle
You catch each seed
And collect
And reform them back
Back into their original shape
Or even slightly different
But at least close
You would have grasped
The full meaning of my words
The dandelion head
And the poem would be complete
And so would I.

There is a warm glow and utter contentment when a poem is understood.

Unknown

The Goose and the Common

This is a wonderful and very poignant poem written during the 1700s and was a protest against English enclosures. 3 centuries later and we still have the wealthy owning great swathes of open countryside and wilderness that is prohibited for the rest of us to enjoy!
Shared by Jason Conway

The law locks up the man or woman
Who steals the goose from off the common
But leaves the greater villain loose
Who steals the common from off the goose.
The law demands that we atone
When we take things we do not own
But leaves the lords and ladies fine
Who take things that are yours and mine.
The poor and wretched don't escape
If they conspire the law to break
This must be so, but they endure
Those who conspire to make the law.
The law locks up the man or woman
Who steals the goose from off the common
And geese will still a common lack
Till they go and steal it back.

Clare Walters

The Keeper of Secrets

The Keeper of Secrets
Morphing on its axis, the illuminated orb
shines down upon the street below,
Never telling, it is witness to events that the human eye
does not see…cannot see, for they are weighed down by slumber.
An anchor in the sky, it watches……without judgement,
its presence calming to those that are captured by its aura.
For it is the keeper of secrets.

Katherine Grace Hyslop

The peace of a Sunday

The peace of a Sunday
trickles through my veins and
laps at my nerve-endings.

It feels OK. It could be OK..
Despite routine-attempts to resist,
Negativity pulses-by.

"You're not really one of us" I hear It explain.
Capable of positive-action, this one
Selects its victims with care and attention.

(It will feed from that one later).
It has them - as a hyena may -
(that's why I am not 'in the fray'),
variously around, intended fodder.

Fodder for play, 'Play-thing'; Quite a collapsible feast of horror!
It never quite understood this Warrior,
("now bite down hard on this").

Derek Dohren

The Purpose of Life

Chaos theory at Gloucester Quays
is once again subverted
as down in the South China Seas
a typhoon is averted.
I reflect on this as my 12-ton bus
runs over a butterfly
the real purpose of life for us
is in learning how to die.

Bolsheviks storming the Winter Palace.
Those grassy knolls of downtown Dallas.

Being human's a tough gig though
spent musing on life's events
ponder long and watch them grow
have they all been Heaven sent?
I reflect on this at the terminus
and again, as I cruise on by
the real purpose of life for us
is in learning how to die.

That failed trial with Crystal Palace.
Strictly Come Dancing with Shirley Ballas.

Kuma San

There's a Buddha in the garden

Sitting under a tree.
He protects the spiders
Hiding in the leaves.
The butterflies adore him
The flowers are his crown.
He watches at the sunrise
He's still when it goes down.
There's a Buddha in the garden
Through sun and wind and rain
You'll find him sitting cross legged
His face betrays no pain.
The birds alight upon him
Small frogs sit at his feet
The Buddha in the garden
is the place where creatures meet.

Annalisa Jackson

There's a demon roaming in the darkness of the night,

Breathing hot, fetid breath on slumbering forms.

Back rounded and bony, spine jutting in spikes
beneath black skin, leathery and pitted as he leans over,

And with claws extended he hovers;

Spittle emerging from a mouth filled with yellowing
and decayed fangs.

A chuckle devoid of humour splits the quiet of the night,
like a blunt cleaver that tears meat from bone.

Beneath his unwavering, contemptuous gaze movement begins,

They stir and wake, and while he hides

He watches with one eye behind dark curtains.

With limbs in need of muscles to be stretched they hobble,
gradually rotating head, arms, shoulders, back,

As the staggering hobble gradually becomes a firm, confident pace.

As they reach for a cup he creeps in slowly,

With water poured, gulped into dry mouth

He touches their shoulder,

Claws surprisingly light.

They do not turn his way but freeze on the spot

as he gently strokes their face,

Beginning now to whisper, voice raw as if vocal cords sit tight,
like violin wires

That are scraped with metal, and rasp their protest in dry
and vile words of malicious intent.

On the edge of hearing

Body stiffens, drink abruptly poured down sink, hand cuffs mouth

Light switch clicked off they hurry between darkened rooms

With sighs of relief their body lowers and legs swing
up and under covers

And now the demon smiles, eyes hungry, bright in the dark
like twin moons in a starless sky

And with self-satisfied smirk climbs in beside them.

Kuma San

There's a monk in the kitchen

Sitting very still
He looks as if he's praying
I'm not sure what to do!

I know not where he's come from
Or if he's been there long
He's sitting in my kitchen
As if there's nothing wrong.

Maroon about his shoulders
orange at his chest,
He looks as if he's happy
On my kitchen floor at rest.

So do I go and join him,
Walk in sit down and say,
Good morning monk,
You're welcome here
Have you come to pray?

It's all a little early,
The day has scarce begun
The monk has caught me on the hop,
Though I'm disinclined to run.

I'm thinking on reflection
It might be kinda nice,
To sit a while in silence,
Perhaps gain sage advice.

There's a monk in my kitchen
Sitting with his beads
I think the thing he's waiting for
may very well be me.

Becky Who

There's a poem

There's a poem in your eyes
I caught a glimpse as our paths crossed
You looked elsewhere, a little lost
Frowning about the everyday
Missing house keys, bills to pay
But deep down I saw a sadness that ached
To be given words before it's too late.

There's a poem in your mouth
Yes, the booze is talking for you
Tongue loosened by a drink or two
But somewhere in your wine-soaked words
A heart-felt message can be heard
And treasured, to give to life some meaning
Far beyond a pleasant drunken evening.

There's a poem on your lips
There may be so much left to say
But there the words will have to stay
As now we are alone at last
The time for speech has surely passed
And if your lips quiver with things unsaid
Let us put them to other tasks instead

There's a poem in my mind
The moment I first saw your face
The words began to fall in place
But art, like love, can lose its way
As time slips by, I know some day
This poem will be all that's left for me
To hold and keep you safe in memory.

Ben Poppy

The Supermarket

I'm working in a supermarket,
A cashier on the checkouts
Stocking up the shelves
Surrounded by masks, hand wash
and gloves
A sometimes-panicked crowd

They stand in a queue
Two metres apart
Before being guided in
by a security guard
Just as I'm about to start

First, it's NHS staff and carers
Because they have other places
to be
Clapped every Thursday evening
Because their work is key

I'm working in a supermarket
A cashier on the checkouts
Stocking up the shelves
Surrounded by masks, hand wash
and gloves
A sometimes-panicked crowd

A woman is left confused, after
having shopped for five people

Another has a trolley full to the brim,
for no one but herself

Hands had found their way through
the plastic, and into a cage
Before I could get anything out onto
the shelf

And it's hard not to be belittled
When you're the face that is feeding a
rage
But, maybe that is something that can
change
 In this ridiculous era
This locked down age

I'm working in a supermarket
A cashier on the checkouts
Stocking up the shelves
Surrounded by masks, hand wash
and gloves
A sometimes-panicked crowd

There's litter inside the trolleys
There's litter inside the mind
Left over by conspiracy theories
And what has been left behind

There's a need for cleanliness
There's a need for one in one out
There's a need for humour
In this nightmare, in this head full
of doubt

I'm working in a supermarket
A cashier on the checkouts
Stocking up the shelves
Surrounded by masks, hand wash
and gloves
A sometimes-panicked crowd

There are complaints in aisle three
Empty shelves in aisle seven
Vans are loaded and ready to go
As shoplifters converge on aisle eleven

There's a spillage in aisle two
A freezer breakdown on aisle four
Shoplifters are grabbed by security guards, And pushed behind closed doors

I'm working in a supermarket
A cashier on the checkouts
Stocking up the shelves
Surrounded by masks, hand wash and gloves
A sometimes-panicked crowd

Alcohol is the essential item
We all need somewhere to go
When we sit inside and bury our head,
In another Netflix show

More food is being consumed
As the floods have grown higher
As an argument starts with a customer exempt,
Being called a liar

A supermarket full of pandemic saints
Who tell you how it should be
Pointing out non-masked devils
While picking out their tea

There's action where is never happens
In unexpected places

As I look outside the front door
And see a queue of faces

There's a rush for toilet roll
A rush for flour and alcohol
There's a rush for eggs
From the outside looking in
It's as if we've lost our soul

I'm working in a supermarket
A cashier on the checkouts
Stocking up the shelves
Surrounded by masks, hand wash and gloves
A sometimes-panicked crowd.

Alby Stockley

The White Discussion

Man down, they said
but it's ok we don't know the whole story
let's check out his previous history
I say you can't justify another casualty

Man down, they said
but it's ok, his previous convictions
mean he don't have a say
I say criminality don't lessen your humanity

Man down, they said
but It's ok 'cos he had a bad cheque
the whole world watched
screaming get off his spine, get off his neck

Man down, we said
you don't get to do that
they said we can understand your pain
but can you sanitise that?

Can you tone down your voice?
can you quieten your pain?
we don't want it spilling
out your neighbourhood again
can you please not mention shit like white fragility
'cos, you know we don't see colour
and we're all about equality

If you keep inside your homes
we'll have some more discussions
where we'll look into the matter
before we whitewash the blood splatter
we promise there'll be change
but first let's reassign the blame.

Drea MacMillan

38

She shut the bud
(the size of a baby's fist)
behind flesh-coloured doors
Never saw it bloom
Only imagined each petal

dropping to the floor

dark red as clotted blood

Atrophied stem, an empty vase
Withered petals, pooled and lifeless
like geriatric skin and lost chances.

Kay Hamblin

Having just joined, feels a bit pushy to be putting something else out so soon, but this is in response to recent events. Had planned to attend the vigil for Sarah tonight, but it was cancelled. This is a very clumsy attempt to put some of how I feel 'out there'.

This woman feels...

…angry
At another life taken
Violence enacted
Horror and loss

…afraid
For her daughters
For all girls and women
For herself

…outraged
At liberties taken
Arrogant assumptions
Casual slurs

…exhausted
By a problem denied
By nothing changing
By 'just get over it'

…hopeful
With our coming together
Things WILL get better
Won't they?

Ivor Daniel

Too many Etonians

on the playing fields of State
preening with entitlement
while others stand and wait.

Tish Camp

Touching Carpaccio

Delicate, sharp cut, like a loose skein of iridescent flesh
lying still in ribboned stress
on boards of her own philosophies.

In antipasto of her life
she is olive, vinegars of balsamic brown trickled
over loose luscious leaves of green
never proportionately bound.

Dark red meat as if a dangerous paint
warning in sinews cut out
tribal appreciation of power
adoration of skin and lips

thinly sliced, roses form in her breast
alone, aromatic, prophetic of wild horses
she is ready and perfectly dressed.

Charlie Markwick

Tournous-Darré

My sleep's settled not fitful
yet the chiming church
breaks my dreams.
Lying sharp awake I listen.
The night is absolutely still.
stepping out of bed
I window frame myself.
It's three o'clock.
The heat of day is gone of course,
a gentle breeze is cool
caressing sleepy skin.
Heavy on the air the scent,
that smell the dew shares with us
when it settles on the grass.
A perfect moment in my life.

I wake again
the ancient village bell,
tells me now, it's four.

Again, I step up to the silent night
but now it's not,
faintly on the air
a keen old rooster
is proclaiming that it's day.
All around there are other birdsongs
gone is that dewy perfume,
the adolescent sun
now prances round
the blades of grass.
What holds my eyes, though,
is the gold
gilded swathes,

ancient yellow, artist's strokes
sunflowers yelling
telling me to start my day.

Tournous-Darré – 27/07/20

Julian Roger Horsfield

Tree People

There are those who live in the woods,
burn sticks and twigs and grope for nettles
for their tea, sister, brother I have love
of thee.

And by the side of the thorny hedge
is a byre and a copse, where badgers dig,
where rabbits and foxes trundle
now under fire by the porky vandals.

And in the trees are lovely folk, and no
I don't care if they drink or smoke,
They are the ones of whom is writ
They faced down the corporation shits.

And though I am not amongst their number
their's the glory and the thunder,
I only hope there is a God ~
although it often seems there's not.

Between Heaven's high beech and oak
they can camp and rest and toke,
they are the best of English folk.

Matty Blades

Versace shirt

You looked down on me when I was at my lowest
But just like you I am no less than flesh and bone
We all have a path, a long winding road with hurdles
But some of us have been destroyed by the madness
A life that has been beset with demons and trauma
Have you ever had to fight demons in the middle of the day?
Yes, you look down on me
But there is only one reason for me to look up you
See on concrete floor here I lay, homeless
Not begging, just trying to sleep it all away
I see the burning in your eyes, as you bite on your hot dog
Ketchup all down your Versace shirt -
I'm guessing the twinkle has returned to mine.

Simon Townsend

Virus
Should really be writing something about the solstice but this just fell out...

Changing
rearranging
Shape shifting
Life disrespecting
infecting scores
Could be you and yours
On an ill will blown
Makes Ingress to your homes
Air borne transmission
Unseen in some
Others intensive
Breathing unable
Life unstable
Still, it changes
many facets
Sped up
What comes next
Medicine stretched
Evolve to confound
Man's new battleground

Darcy Royce

War is War

You think we care what name you gave it,
the reason behind the first strike,
ignorance, greed and pride - legacy,
yours to own and explain,
how could you - refrain from an invitation,
temptation, to retrain your mind,
your arms,
the kind that takes and chokes,
into the bloody freedom fighter,
to mend them broken bones,
on one side and the other,
why pick a side,
just stop, and take yourself out
altogether,
into ice cold or hellish hot weather,
see how it feels,
on either side of the barricade,
without a guide,
just serenade - bombs, guns, charred bodies,
there you go...
History is teaching you a lesson,
it will be painful,
it will hurt you and everyone else,
yet you insist,
sadistic swine,
to put our children's back up to a wall,
have you not learned anything?
And I mean,
ANYTHING,
at all!?

John Aubry

What day is it

Monday morphs to Tuesday
Wednesday follows suit
Thursday is quite boring
With Friday in pursuit
Saturday starts the weekend
Sunday ends the week
Monday morphs to Tuesday
My life is on repeat.

Gabby Wiest

Whispering Thoughts

I feel the stillness
of your mind
your untroubled heart
peaceful and calm
pure beauty
like the silence
of the night.

I hear the echoes
of the wind
like whispering thoughts
shouting in the air
that your ink lives
beyond
ten thousand years.

Trevor Valentine

Winter Solstice - The Oak King

The oak tree captured in its rings
Every memory of every year
For an eternity it seemed
And even the ragged times
Were caught safely
Like stardust
In a softened leather glove
Its roots gripped the earth host
Like gnarled toes;
Look carefully
And you can see its eyes
With ageing brows
Weather beaten
Wisdom engrained
It cradles the memories
And keeps them ever safe.

Lucia Daramus

Winter-Spring
to Faye Vick

It snows
as after holidays
with snails
the whole world is a shell
you can feel the smell of
resurrection in the grave
It snows
lambs - ramping as after a Sardonic dream
within the swarming of the astral rain -
kneel before the holy Easter
It snows
with entries in Jerusalem
with palm-tree branches
thorny crown of blood .
a metaphysical corner
takes shape in me
the snow becomes one flesh with the rain
like a transcendental kiss.
on the shrine the rain is to break
It snows
with crucifixion
it is winter-spring...
and - I - look out of the sky window
at - my - friend eternity...eternity...
per aspera ad astra!
.....and....behind us only fragile tearing souls.

I wrote this poem Winter-Spring after my friend in Gloucestershire committed suicide. She was a beautiful artist, and she suffered with metal health.
I am myself also with paranoid schizophrenia and Asperger's syndrome, but I try to convert my problems in art, writing, creativity. The poem is talking about one day of us when a metaphysical corner is blooming in our heart.

Morgan 'I'm-not-a-poet' Rye

You pollute me

How do I hate thee? Let me count the ways.
Whether 'tis nobler to punch you in the eye
than entertain the thoughts in my mind?
Care not I.
For your voice booms in every room of my house,
Hour upon day upon month and more,
Deep into night,
Boom, bang, yell, crash.
Your presence shakes the air,
Infected with your smell and I long to be elsewhere.
While the town sleeps you shout into black,
And I ask, plead.
You say all the right things but do not alter.
I cannot make sense of things.
You pollute me to desperate exhaustion.
I fall, I hurt, I cry,
So desperate am I.

Still, you play and yell and quake my life,
Nothing exists to stop you.
What is my head without its ache, a smile, work, sleep?
I need to sleep.
Tremors take my body,
Pain fills it with vitriol.
Eye for an eye...
I'll bake that pie,
And shove it in your face white hot.
Noise, noise, noise tears at my skin.
When will it stop?
Would there was a power to drag you by the heels,
Chain them to a brutal monster machine,
Alone with a sound bigger than you,
Day upon month and more.
To feel what it is that you do.

Suz Winspear   29/11/20

Zoom
A poem that I wrote tonight . . .

We meet online, in tiny rectangles.
We talk, perform our poetry and prose
to silent applause,
appreciation muted –
we're at the limits of technology,
an unexpected sound could break the internet.
And we're judging one another's homes,
wondering at backgrounds
and the pictures on the walls.
Afterwards we chat,
speak to familiar faces
that we haven't seen for months
outside these rectangles on screens.
It ends, it switches off
and we're alone again, in silence –
the overwhelming silence.

The Poets

Adele Ojier Jones

27   Circadian Riddle

A member of The Poetry Society (UK), Adèle writes creatively as Ogiér Jones. She has four collections of poems, including Beyond the Blackbird Field (Ginninderra Press, 2016), and three chapbooks in the Ginninderra Press Pocket Poets series. She appears in numerous anthologies and is a regular contributor to e-poetry journals. A new collection with her Irish poems is due for publication in 2022. Blogging from time to time, she follows poetry forums at: **https://www.facebook.com/adele.ogierjones.**

Akon Nouhry

18   A Prayer

Nouhr-Dine D. Akondo writes drama and poetry both in French and English. Senior Lecturer of his home university, he lives in Lomé the capital city of Togo, West Africa. He is a co-organiser of the "Festival International des Lettres et Arts" (FESTILARTS) at the University of Lomé. He writes and draws much of his subject matter from African culture and history and is interested in Contemporary World socio-economic and political issues.

His poems have been published in a number of African poetry magazines, namely Afro-poésie (Online), Best New African Poetry 2016, Contemporary Poetry from Africa (2019), COVID-19 DIARY: World's Anthology of Poetry (2020), I Can't Breathe: A Poetic Anthology of Fresh Air (2020).

Alby Stockley

39	Fibroids
123	The White Discussion

Alby Stockley is a poet, Spoken Word performer and Textile Artist based in Kent. Her writing is mainly biographical touching on hard hitting subjects. She has been described as an empathic and emotive performer.

Alby has featured at Spoken Word London's Anti hate festival, Maidstone's Fringe festival, Squawkers and Worcester Pride with her son, Elric as well as featuring at Rusty Goats Poetry Corner and GPS's Raised Voices for women's international day. She has recently had a poem published in S.O.S SURVIVING SUICIDE a collection of poems that may save a life.

Alby can be found hosting and performing at POCO POETS in Rochester Kent.

Annalisa Jackson

115   There's a demon roaming in the darkness of the night

Annalisa is a freelance writer and photographer at TBB Freelancing Services. When she's not providing work for others from her corner of the sitting-room she has claimed as an office she is an author and poet who writes and performs as 'The Beanie Bard' owing to her trademark hat.

Having participated in her first open mic in April of 2019 she has gone on to take part in multiple slams with her first win in May 2021. Her second children's book 'In The Land Of The Boogaloo' is being released next Spring with her first 'The Sky Painter' available on Amazon.

Hopefully a poetry collection may follow one day if she ever sorts herself out. You can find her on Instagram or Facebook at
https://www.facebook.com/ajacksonauthor/
https://www.instagram.com/annalisa_jackson_author
or her websites
https://www.tbbfreelancing.com
https://www.thebeaniebard.com

Ann-Marie kurylak

42   Futile

Ann-Marie Kurylak would describe herself as a poet of the heart as her work stems from raw emotion. Originally from Gloucester in England, she now lives in Tilburg in the Netherlands with her Dutch partner and spends her free time exploring her Dutch home and learning the language.

Ann D Stevenson

58   Lockdown

Ann is retired and living in Gloucestershire, UK. She has had a few poems published on line, under the name of Ann D Stevenson, not to be confused with that well known poet, Anne Stevenson.

Becky Who

47   If you liked my poetry
85   Poetic Warning
118   There's a poem

Becky is a British poet living in France, writing and performing in both English and French. Trained as a musician and musicologist, she now teaches English as a foreign language to French students in Grenoble, often using music, poetry and slam as pedagogical tools. Her first love is performance poetry, and she has been a finalist in several slam tournaments, both onstage and online, in English and French. She has also worked with French slam poets to translate their work (complete with rhyme!). Married with two children, she is working on her first poetry chapbook.
Facebook: Becky Who Poetry
Instagram: @beckywhopoetry

Ben Poppy

119   The Supermarket

Ben Poppy is a playwright/film maker and poet, who has recently had his second collection of poetry published, **We Are Frankenstein**. He deals with a variety of subjects, from mental health, social issues and describing the ongoings within the city of London which he loves, and where he currently resides. His second collection mainly deals with life under lockdown and all that came with it.

Brian Reid

101   Sunrise on Cherhill

Brian Reid is a writer/performer/storyteller just trying to make some sense of it all. It still doesn't but the ride has been an interesting one, for him at least. Grandfather, MC, community activist , cancer survivor and still committed to growing old with a bit of panache. His first collection is planned for 2022.

Carol Sheppard

17   Apple
82   Phone Box
98   Step forward to the new year…

Carol is a poet and playwright living in the Forest of Dean. Her poetry has been published in various journals and anthologies and her plays have been performed in the UK, New Zealand and Hawaii. Much of her poetry is inspired by the beautiful landscape where she lives and the people she meets.

Catrice Greer

32   Cygnus, Monogamous

Residing in Baltimore, Maryland USA, Catrice Greer is a 2021 Pushcart Prize Nominee.

She served in November 2020 as a Poet-In-Residence for Cheltenham Poetry Festival (UK).

Presently, Catrice is a Guest Editor for IceFloe Press and a Guest Poetry reviewer for Fevers of the Mind blog.

Her work has been published in digital literary magazines, international anthologies, blogs, and local newsletters.

She is currently working towards publishing her first collection.

Please feel free to explore her website
www.catricegreer.com

Charlie Markwick

79   Paroles de Joie
128   Tournous-Darré

Charlie Markwick is a Gloucestershire born spoken word performer, poet and storyteller. He grew up in the Cotswolds and now lives in the Haute-Pyrénées. A long time GPS member, Charlie was for a period, poet in residence at Gloucester Library. In 2019 he published his first book of poems "**Orienteering**", pieces from his show of the same name. He has been included in the GPS Anthologies: "Magic" (2019), and "The Trawler" (2020). Also, in "Today I feel Hawaii" (2019) edited by the then Gloucestershire Poet Laureate Brenda Read-Brown. Two of his poems were published on Good Dadhood,
https://gooddadhood.com/2020/05/24/two-poems-by-charlie-markwick/
His poems about dementia have been included in resources created by the NHS. In 2020 Bream Community Library produced videos of him performing his poetry for their Poetry Box Project,
https://www.breamcommunitylibrary.co.uk/charlie-markwick-2
Charlie is currently working with musicians and visual artists around the world on a project combining their compositions and his words.

Chloë Jacquet

65   My Sofa is Missing You

Chloë Jacquet is a multicultural, multifaceted spoken word artist based in Gloucestershire. She was 2017 Oxford Hammer & Tongue slam champion and twice reached the semi-finals of the National Slam Finals at the Royal Albert Hall.

With a preference for straight talking and a penchant for rhymes and opinions, Chloë's poetry is both entertaining and meaningful. Her work deals with a wide variety of subjects, ranging from workplace discrimination and mental health, to the pressures placed on modern men, via her short-term relationship with a biscuit.

Chloë thinks name dropping is really uncool. As well as her own headline slots, she has supported artists such as Elvis McGonagall, Joelle Taylor and Hollie McNish and her work has featured several times on the BBC.

Her first collection Take It By The Line is published by Black Eyes Publishing UK.

Chloë can be found on social media using the handle @ChloeJPoetry.

Chris Barber

41   From Intake to Uptake

Chris Barber is sixty and grows increasingly grumpy, according to his children, despite the beauty of his surroundings in the market town of Newent, where he's been resident for over twenty-five years.

Clare Walters

111   The Keeper of Secrets

Clive Oseman

68   Not in my Name
90   Shakespeare in the Age of Doom and Zoom

Clive Oseman is a Swindon based Brummie spoken word artist, comedian, satirist and promoter.

His third collection, **It Could Be Verse**, was published by Black Eyes in 2020 and promptly caused a pandemic.

His one man, show, "**What if they laugh at me?**" will probably trigger an apocalypse, so best to catch it early.

Darcy Royce

56   Jennie in a Bottle
133   War is War

Darcy Royce is an English poet, based in Wiltshire, who is passionate about advocating for mental health, and unlocking the inner healer through creative writing. She writes therapeutic poetry based on her background in Psychology, clinical hypnotherapy and coaching.

Darryl John

38 End

Darryl John is a passionate Welsh poet who has been writing poetry since the age of thirteen. His style is very forthright and tackles many controversial issues. Darryl writes from personal experience and is very candid concerning his mental state, He believes that poetry is still a valid creative art and that it should evoke a reaction in the reader.

Darryl has studied poetry with the help of Nigel Mcloughlin and Angela France at the University of Gloucestershire. Darryl prefers to write free verse but feels that learning the forms first really helped him understand what structure was about, before he challenged the norms. Darryl uses a lot of concrete detail and is always looking to describe something very differently from how it would be expected. He also takes great pleasure in twisting the ending into something unexpected.

He has written a poem a day for the last year, just to see if he could. For Darryl poetry is therapy.

Derek Dohren

48   I Just Don't Know
113   The Purpose of Life

Derek Dohren was last spotted heading north by north-west and (at the time of writing) is believed to be driving his buses across the Isle of Skye in Scotland. God only knows what they make of him up there. Ugly rumour has it that at some point, perhaps sooner rather than later, he will return to terrorising the gentle fairy folk of the Forest of Dean and acting as if he never buggered off in the first place.

Until such times you can avail yourself of his two poetry collections, **'Everything Rhymes with Orange'** ISBN-13 978-1913195038 and **'Wasp in My Cockpit'** ISBN-13 978-1913195137, both published by Black Eyes Publishing UK. Signed copies are available at Derek's website at, **www.derekdohren.com/apps/webstore**

Devlin Wilson

52   I see you
99   Sunday with the Dead

Devlin Wilson is a long-time member of the GPS who lives and works in Gloucester. He also contributed to the Trawler 2020.

DrayZera

45   Hexagonal Diagonal
93   Shapeshifters Lullaby

DrayZera is a spoken word performing poet, podcaster, director and music artist. DrayZera began in 2016 and since then have racked up over 200 performances across four countries including San Francisco's 10th Annual Beat Poetry Festival. DrayZera released his debut poetry collection 'Broken Circuitboard' with the later release 'Secret Diaries' pamphlet in 2017. In 2019, 'Psycho Lucy' - A Cinematic Spoken Word Film Series - Mixing spoken word and horror shot in the historical city of Bath. DrayZera released music with 'Cut Them Loose' and 'King Is Dead' in 2020. In 2021, "The Journey/The Ascendant" was released. The journey continues with further creative and masked artistry to come...

Drea MacMillan

124   38

Andrea Macmillan lives in the quaint town of Malmesbury in Wiltshire with her ever faithful rescue dog Jack. She has always loved writing and began her first novel at the tender age of seven after being inspired by Enid Blyton's 'The Wishing Chair'. She is a passionate reader and has an eclectic taste in books from the classics to modern African American literature. Her ideal way to spend the day is by the beach with her nose in a book. Her love of reading and writing paved the way to her career as a copywriter and she now runs her own business, Drea Macmillan Social Marketing.

Her earlier work focuses on her experience as a domestic violence survivor. Nature and her love of travel feature strongly in her more recent work which explore the themes of lust, love and loss.

A powerful performance poet, Drea has headlined at several poetry events in Cheltenham, Swindon and Gloucester.
IG @drea.macmillan
Facebook @dreamacmillan
www.dreamacmillan.com

Franchesa Kirkpatrick

57   Leaving Darkness in Pine Trees Burning

Franchesa is a Nashville, Tennessee native world traveller. She has been a writer and storyteller from a young age. Franchesa has had poems published in the Library of Poetry, Vanderbilt Ingram Cancer Center Anthologies and online magazines such as Medium and Views Hound. She reads at Poetry in the Brew, Literature Cafe Global and in Poetry Zooms around the world.
Franchesawolfe@hotmail.com
www. Youtube.com/Franchesavideos
www.Instagram.com/Franchesapic
Twitter.com/Angel2Music

Gabby A. Wiest

31   Creature of the Night
40   Forbidden Love
135   Whispering Thoughts

My poetry book is all about thoughts, feelings, emotion and longing for affection .it is poetry for the soul, and speaks to your mind and heart. What is most important to you, and how it will affect people around you.

Gabby a Filipina by birth, lives in Canada where she is married to Canadian, Reg Wiest, writer/photographer.

Gemma Crow

64   My ripples, My pond
86   Potential too alluring

Jewellery Maker – TV Presenter – Poet
www.gemmacrow.com

Ian Paulin

35   Edge of dark and light

ian paulin hails from Tasmania. He has been an Artist, Academic, Community Worker and Activist for over 40 years. He's campaigned for peace, to save rivers and wilderness, and worked in community programs with youth and adult homelessness, at risk and survivor groups, anti-bullying, disability development programs, community education, public philosophy, and philosophy in schools. He holds a Masters in Public Policy and politics, and is completing a PhD in the same discipline @ Utas. He has 8 music albums on Apple Music and Spotify and has performed at top music events in Australia and OS.
https://www.facebook.com/ian.paulin1
https://music.apple.com/au/artist/ian-paulin/591183445
https://open.spotify.com/artist/3pKYXtLatnS1lP03YLZz8G
https://www.youtube.com/channel/UCxHs1KRh3lN4FlAnfFV_Eyg

Isobel May

80 Peace

Aged 23, in a time of turmoil both around the world and within my own life, peace came and went like the tide. The idea for Peace came from finally hearing a silence in my head that I hadn't heard for so long. I hope to have more moments like this and to continue writing and sharing my work.
Isobel Hancocks.

Ivor Daniel

126 Too many Etonians

Ivor studied English at Southampton University, then took up a career in Youth & Community Work. He now does English tutoring for GCSE and A-level students.

His poems have appeared in A Spray of Hope (an anthology of pandemic poetry published by Liverpool University), wildfire words (the ezine of Cheltenham Poetry Festival), Steel Jackdaw Magazine, Writeresque Magazine and iamb ~ wave seven.

Ivor would like to thank @LitSciHub, Cheltenham Poetry Festival and Gloucestershire Poetry Society for their energising online workshops and poetry readings.
@IvorDaniel

Jason Conway

60   Melness Sunset
103   Tape my mouth

Jason Conway is a passionate eco-poet and professional daydreamer (freelance design professional, writer, poet, artist, photographer and creative mentor) based in Stroud, Gloucestershire. Drawing inspiration from social issues, mental health and the transformative power of nature, his mission is to encourage people to make a difference in the world, for the protection of the planet and the wellbeing of its custodians. Jason crafts design, art, words and photography to educate, challenge and inspire people to take positive action.

He is a Co-Director of The Gloucestershire Poetry Society. Jason's debut collection '**Phoenix Rises**' was published in 2018. He's performed at the 2000 Trees Festival, headlined at the Gloucestershire Poetry Festival and The Space In-Between Festival and has been published in The Blue Nib, Poetry Bus and The Poetry Village magazines.
Facebook @jasonconwaypoetry
Instagram @jasonleeconway
Twitter @daydreamacademy
www.jasonconwaypoetry.co.uk
www.thedaydreamacademy.com

John Aubry

134   What day is it

https://sites.google.com/view/poemsnpercussion/home?authuser=0

Jonathan Robert Muirhead (1978 ~ 2020)

83   Poem – Preacher – Draft 1

Jonathan had two poems featured posthumously in the Trawler 2020. This draft poem, possibly his last, was posted within the time frame for the Trawler 2021.

Josephine Lay

106   **The Abscission of Trees** (first draft)

Josephine Lay is a poet and author living between Gloucester and Cheltenham. She has a jnt. BA(Hons) in Creative Studies in Eng. & English Lit. and an MA in Creative Writing from Bath Spa University.

During 2018 Josephine suffered two falls, both resulting in concussion and a period of post-concussion syndrome. This precipitated Josephine into writing poetry and she joined The Gloucestershire Poetry Society (GPS). She became host of 'Squawkers' – a monthly poetry event in Cheltenham and since the Pandemic, Josephine hosts the online Zoom event, 'Crafty Crows', which has become highly successful and International. In Jan 2020 Josephine became Director of Operations for the GPS.

Josephine's most recent poetry collection is entitled **A Quietrus** (2021). Her previous collections, **Unravelling** (2019) and **Inside Reality** (2018), all published by 'Black Eyes', and available from Amazon and to order from your usual bookseller throughout the world. For signed copies, go to the 'Black Eyes Shop…
https://www.blackeyespublishinguk.co.uk/shop
https://www.blackeyespublishinguk.co.uk/josephine-lay-poet

Julian Roger Horsfield

130   Tree People

Julian doesn't smoke or drink, but he once did take a magic mushroom. And that could explain a few things. He's often in the bluebells where he insists on writing poems, drinks tea and eats cheese and tomato sandwiches".

Katherine Grace Hyslop

112   The Peace of a Sunday

Katherine Grace Hyslop: Born in glorious Filey, Yorkshire, I wandered around England. In 2000 I settled in Stroud with my amazing 'children'. Since before I started school, I have been writing the occasional poem; those very early poems were prayer-like.

I have enjoyed Creative Writing Workshops periodically; and more recently have been a member of the Gloucestershire Poetry Society, which, to my mind is usually a fun and enriching experience. I have some minor (esoteric) publications in the field of Health Promotion/Public Health.

I play the piano, and sometimes I compose a melody; most likely inspired by a person I care about or an unusual event, for example.

Kay Hamblin

125   This woman feels...

Kelly Owen

16		Any other day
76		One very fucked up "I love you!"

Keren Hermon

44		Government
46		Hollow Man

I used to write verse when I was young, either snippy and funny or tightly wound and angry. Then I spent some years on short stories. I came to poetry proper at 70 when I discovered the GPS and much enjoyed learning and practicing with their encouragement. I think I'm getting better as I go along.

Kezzabelle Ambler

36   **Emergency Muse**
97   **Spellings**

Published performance poet, Kezzabelle Ambler, playfully weaves her wit and wisdom to connect with depth, warmth and comedic observation. Her boundless love of words and people radiates through her fifth book 'Permission To Speak' poems of love, mischief, green issues, mental health, racism and nature.

Kezzabelle runs 'Weaving Words' creative writing workshops in the community, festivals and in mental health wards. She helps all ages to voice their story to express their thoughts and feelings hoping their pen becomes a tool for life.

She curates and hosts the 'Kezzabelle Poet Weaving Words Podcast, her 'Spectrum On Air' radio show and 'The Kezzabelle Connection', entertaining diverse audiences with eclectic poets, bards, musicians and storytellers she meets on her travels.
Her uplifting and motivational talks and spoken word shows exude passion and energy baring all through her craft, blessing and inspiring whoever crosses her path.
www.kezzabelle.co.uk.

Kuma San

28	Cocooned on warm sofa
114	There's a Buddha in the garden
117	There's a monk in the kitchen

Kuma San lives a few miles outside Gloucester. She is a novice, lay Buddhist priest and currently runs popular, weekly online meditation sessions, using a collection of resonating instruments. Kuma is an instinctive composer, percussionist and musician, playing singing bowls, large gong and cymbals as well as rainmakers, sticks and mouth sounds to create a deeply moving, meditative experience.

Recently Kuma has turned her creativity towards words. Her poetry echoes her music and speaks of her joy of nature, her gentleness and compassion for all beings. She's become an active member of the local poetry scene, and took part in the GPS 'Raised Voices' celebration of 'International Women's Day' at St Mary de Crypt, Gloucester, in February 2020. The poem she read on that day, 'Forget Me Not 2', is in The Trawler 2020.

Laura Grevel

13   A Man on the Bus
22   Ballad of Burg Rappotenstein

Laura Grevel is a performance poet, fiction writer and blogger. Originally from Texas, she has performed in Texas, Austria, Switzerland, and England. A proud member of DIY Poets and Poets Against Racism Nottingham and the Gloucestershire Poetry Society, her work is eclectic, tackling the immigrant experience, narratives, politics, and character sketches. Her written work has been published in podcasts, zines, anthologies and newspapers. A number of her poetry performances can be viewed on her YouTube channel. Her latest collaborative YouTube video is called "Girl Walking Across Europe" by Poets For Refugees, created as an Act of Welcome for refugees.
YouTube:
https://www.youtube.com/channel/UCx1dH7vxwIIjVxPd8fs_9xQ
Blog: https://lgrevel.wordpress.com/
Website: http://lgrevel.org/
Twitter: https://twitter.com/LauraGrevel/
FB: https://www.facebook.com/LauraHGrevel

Lacey Tidwell

73   Numbers Are Up, So I'm Back in Covid ICU

This was taken from a Facebook entry by Lacey, subsequently reposted. It was originally posted in prose, almost in the form of a letter from a nurse to her patient. The words and story flowed through the piece with some beauty, so much so, that I thought it might deserve an attempt at capturing it as a poem. Only the format has been changed.   Trevor Valentine.

Lacey Tidwell is a Nursing Supervisor at Our Lady of the Lake, a not-for-profit healthcare ministry based in Baton Rouge, Louisiana, USA

Lucia Daramus

137   Winter - Spring

Lucia Daramus is a writer and a poet whose works demonstrate her fascination with archaeology, antiquity, words, colours, and philosophy. Sometimes she paints. Daramus has obsession for colours, words and ideas, she has Asperger's Syndrome and Paranoid Schizophrenia. She has a lot of discussion about the relationship between arts (as poetry and painting) and philosophy with her voices... Mircea Lacatus, a European sculptor, said about Lucia: "she has something from an angel's accuracy and something from the disturbance of a mad human being". Also Irina Petras, literary critic said: 'With her poems in her minds, with the bright face all the time, Lucia Daramus does not let you guess what will be her next step. It is sure her work arouses the curiosity.' In the The Books of The Tens Decade.

Lucia's last studies was with the Oxford University, creative writing, relating biography, autobiography, memoir, having the main tutor Profesor Jeremy Hughes. Also writer - Lecturer Kevan Manwaring, relating to Lucia's works, said "Great stuff, Lucia. Keep going. You have a distinctive voice and vision." -outsidein.

Marilyn Timms

21   **Autumnus: Roman Harvest Goddess**
77   **On Hold**
88   **Realisation**

Marilyn Timms, a writer and artist from Cheltenham, is a great believer in beginner's luck. The first literary competition she entered won her a holiday for two in the Caribbean. Since then, she has been widely published online and in print. Marilyn has read her prizewinning poems and short stories at six Cheltenham Literature Festivals. Her first poetry collection, Poppy Juice, is described by Alison Brackenbury as 'a collection of brave and unexpected adventures, with intoxicating, sometimes threatening colours.'

Two of Marilyn's comedies have reached the stage, the third lies mouldering alongside her novel. Her poems Realisation and On Hold first appeared in Deciphering the Maze (Indigo Dreams, 2020), a collection written in collaboration with her husband of 54 years. Having both survived cancer, they are now facing another adventure together – their new puppy.

Marilyn is co-editor at wildfire words, the publishing arm of Cheltenham Poetry Festival.
https://wildfire-words.com

Matty Blades

25	Blood Stain
87	Rare Marble
131	Versace Shirt

Hi guys, I'm Matty Blades I'm a Swindon born poet who started writing in 2001 after tragically losing my sister. I started writing poetry more as a journal, I had no experience in writing poetry, or understanding of punctuation and my spelling left something to be desired. I always dabbled with art, but writing was another matter, once the pen hit my hand though, that was it, I was off. I prefer to write dark poetry as it allows me to look for a deeper understanding of myself and the world around me. I hope you all in enjoy my poetry. B¿@d€.

Morgan 'I'm-not-a-poet' Rye

33	During a pandemic, in this economy
107	The boards are bare
138	You pollute me

Morgan Rye is a second year published poet and aspiring novelist. Her travels and careers in social provision and engineering both inform on her poetry, her passion for writing social sci-fi and her art.

New to the south-west poetry scene, she does not describe herself as a poet, and explains this in terms of the exceptional skill she has come to admire in others. Her first novel, **Snowball Earth – Quinn**, is due to be published by 'Black Eyes' soon.

Nick Lovell

29   Contact
62   My Generation

Nick Lovell is a full time optimist, part time poet and half arsed anarchist. He has won slams, performed at the Royal Albert Hall, Performed as an open miker, support act, headliner and host at various events both in real time and online and has a book, Ever Since The Accident" published Black Eyes Publishing. He Co-hosts Oooh Beehive in Swindon alongside Clive Oseman.

Nupur Chakrabarty

15   Anew

Nupur Chakrabarty is an Indian poet . She is a post-graduate in Psychology from the University of Delhi. She writes prose also. She writes both prose and poetry in her mother-tongue Bengali too . She is a nature-lover. Her poems have been published in various magazines in India and abroad. Her poems depict life as she sees it.

Polly Stratton

66   My stalwart friend

Polly Stratton, all mum, part teacher, part human rights activist, part pirate. Lives in Stroud in a castle on a hill with Jack, her familiar, and her two, better than humanly possible children. She's not a poet, she's a very naughty girl.

Richard Adkins

30   Covid City

Richard Atkins, BBC broadcaster and journalist has been writing poetry for a decade. His poems are inspired by both urban and rural Gloucestershire.

Robert Lang

50   In-Crowd!

Scott Cowley

53   It's a lonely life

Scott Cowley aka Rusty Goat.
Poet and Performer.
Promoter and Host. Championing all things Mental Health, Opening doors for conversations into difficult subjects (established 2017)
[F] Rusty Goat's Poetry Corner

Simon Townsend

132   Virus

My name is Simon Townsend, I am 50 years old and I am a stonemason (drystone Waller), I live in Cirencester, and have two daughters and a wife (hence the rapidly greying hair).

I am a recent convert to writing poetry (3 years or so) but it has always been in me. I find it is something I 'have' to do when the inspiration hits more than 'I'm going to sit down and write a poem' For me it's a very cathartic thing.

I can sometimes be a bit challenging but not just for the shock value and I tend to have a definite rhythm to my stuff.

Sue Finch

19   A Suitcase for Leaving
78   Overnight
94   Silence

Sue Finch lives with her wife in North Wales.
She tweets at **@soopoftheday**
Her debut collection, **'Magnifying Glass'**, was published in October 2020 with Black Eyes Publishing UK.

Suz Winspear

139   Zoom

Worcestershire Poet Laureate 2016-2017 Suz Winspear is a regular performer on the Worcestershire spoken word scene, hosting, **SpeakEasy**, and **42Worcester**. Her collection, '**The Awkward People** ' was published in 2018, and she is currently putting a new collection together.

Tish Camp

26	Buildings (Haiku)
71	Nubian Queen
96	Slept in My Dress
127	Touching Carpaccio

Tish Camp - London born Trinidadian / Irish feminist published poet, artist and theatre maker. She performs internationally and consciously. She is lipstick, boots, politic and verse! Compared in 2020 to UK spoken word artist Kae Tempest and most recently to black US 'Harlem Renaissance' poet Langston Hughes, Tish Camp brings a modern, lick to her take on fighting against racism and oppression.

She was nominated for the 2019 Gloucestershire Poet Laureate and won a Paper Nations 2020 commission as a marginalised writer for South West England.

Tish has Featured and performed across UK, Scotland, Ireland, Paris, Nashville, Australia, New York, San Francisco, Tokyo and at a plethora of poetry events and open mics.

Her poetical and arts work in 2021 continues with The Poets Live platform, her own poetry workshops, poet mentoring, marketing poetry and arts collaborations across Gloucester (UK) with The Gloucestershire Poet Laureate and her ongoing partnership work with US poetry and arts publisher, **EyePublishEwe.**

Tom Cooke

89   Salmonella Sid Stoker and Chef

I'd probably refer to myself as a slightly aging Boater, author, poet and songwriter: My song writing focuses on Folk style music and lyrics about narrow-boating and the people and history of the Black Country. My ancestors and family are pretty much all around the Black Country especially Rowley Regis and Netherton. Those ancestors include Chain makers, pen makers, miners and Puddlers in the steel industry. All songs are available free of charge on Soundcloud and YouTube under Tom Cooke the Boater.

I have also published a children's novel, **'Living on the Cut'**, under the pseudonym of Krista. Additionally I have published two poetry anthologies, **'From the Fiery Pit'** covering an eccletic mix of social issues, humour and nature.

My YouTube channel is,
https://youtube.com/channel/UCR8tp5sZFCp3cANn-HU32Yw
All soundtracks are currently free on Soundcloud
Check out Tom Cooke on #SoundCloud
https://soundcloud.app.goo.gl/2bp4d

Trevor Valentine

108	The Broken Chord
109	The Dandelion Poem
136	Winter Solstice - The Oak King

Guitarist, singer-songwriter, lately poet-in-training, Trevor Valentine has found a welcome refuge in poetry and poets alike. With an original foundation of English, French and Russian literature, Trevor then hit 60, and realised life isn't a rehearsal, which was about the time his daughter started her new life over in Nashville.

If dreams were to come true, I was getting a message from somewhere, it was now-or-never. Poetry and song-writing is unfortunately not a tap you can just turn on, so, when the water flows, enjoy. So pleased to be included in this collection.

Unknown

110	The Goose and the Common

This is a wonderful and very poignant poem written during the 1700s and was a protest against English enclosures. 3 centuries later and we still have the wealthy owning great swathes of open countryside and wilderness that is prohibited for the rest of us to enjoy!
Shared by Jason Conway

Valerie Hartill

61   My Darling

Valerie Hartill is a retired horse dealer, mother to 5, grandmother to 12 and great grandmother to 1.

She has lived in Gloucestershire for many years.

Valerie has a wicked sense of humour and enjoys words.
She has written many funny little rhymes over the years.

Viva O'Flynn

67   New Life

Viva Andrada O'Flynn shares love, joy, and inspiration with the world. She delights in living an active lifestyle. Always on the go, she juggles tasks as a writer, artist, event specialist, host, and entrepreneur.

Originally from the Philippines, now living in the UK, she is happily married to her husband, John. Viva creates special moments with Love Viva Cakes and Crafts.

Viva was awarded Creative Business of the Year 2019, International Women's Day Top 5 Business Women in the UK 2020, awarded by Women's Business Club. Viva was also one of the top winners of World Humanitarian Drive's COVID Times Poetry Competition representing the Philippines.

Viva is also currently the Global Media Relations Head and Host of Inspiring Millions Show of World Humanitarian Drive. Viva's motto is "let's love life all we can while we still can"
Twitter: https://www.twitter.com/vivaciousviva
Facebook: https://www.facebook.com/pages/category/Food---Beverage/lovevivacakesandcrafts/
Website: https://loveviva.company.site/

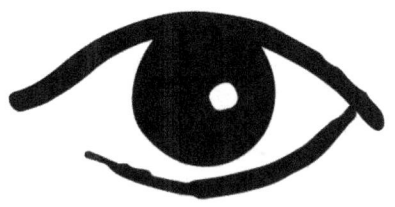

Black Eyes Publishing UK

'Black Eyes' is an independent publisher, based in sight of the cheese-rolling hill in Brockworth, Gloucestershire.

'Publishing from the Edge'

We were established in 2018. Our aims are to produce a small number of exciting, and at times, alternative literature in various genres.

'Quality not Quantity'

blackeyespublishinguk.co.uk

www.ingramcontent.com/pod-product-compliance
Lightning Source LLC
Chambersburg PA
CBHW070103120526
44588CB00034B/2013